TASLEEM PUBLICATIONS
www.expansions.ca

EXPANSIONS -VOLUME Three

First Tasleem Publications edition published 2014. Library of Congress Cataloging-in-Publication Data
Expansions Volume Three – Awakening by Imam Fode Drame
Vancouver, Canada: Tasleem Publications, 2014.

Notes on Translation

In most cases we have attempted to transliterate Arabic words as they are pronounced. Throughout this book, references to the Qur'an are in brackets. These refer to the name of the chapter (*surah*), the chapter number, and then the verse number (*ayah*) for easy reference. When the Prophet Muhammad is mentioned in a paragraph, his mention is followed by the calligraphic symbol for *salla Allahu alayhi wa sallam*, which means, "May the peace and blessings of Allah be upon him."

Contents

HEART TO HEART

Like the two eyes in our head by which we can see the world outwardly, God has also placed two eyes in our heart with which we can see the world inwardly. However as much as our outward eyes can sleep and wake up; our inward eyes also sleep and wake up. While the sleeping with our eyes give sleep and rejuvenation for our body; sleep of the heart brings decay and death to our hearts. Therefore to keep the heart alive it must be awaken permanently preventing it from going to sleep ever after. God says in the Quran:

"Have they not peregrinated in the land so that they may come to acquire a heart by which to understand or ears by which to hear Lo! it is not the eyes in the head that go blind rather what goes blind are the hearts that are in the bosoms" Surah Hajj [The Pilgrimage] (22:46).

A blind heart is one which is not awakened. It is reported that Prophet Muhammad peace be upon him said:

"My eyes sleep but my heart sleeps not likewise the prophets their eyes sleep but their hearts sleep not".

This permanent awakening means perpetual presence with God whether we are sleeping outwardly or not. As for those who have not attained to this full awakening their presence with God is proportionate to their waking moments.

REMEMBRANCE (ذِكْر) AND REFLECTION (فكر)

Of times God invites us to look inwardly within ourselves:
"In there are signs for those who have certitude and within yourselves, won't you see, and in the heavens is your provision and that which you are promised". Surah Ad Dhariyat [The Winds That Scatter] (51:20-22).

This internal look (nazar__نَظَر) through the eyes of the heart leads in two ways:

1. When the inward look (نَظَرَ) leads back to the beginning which comprises the first creation when the Throne (عَرْش) was on water, before the six days of creation, it is known as remembrance (ذِكْر). Therefore whenever God says "remember", he means look through your hearts back to the beginning if you see the beginning then you truly remember God.

2. When the inward look (نَّظَرَ) turns forward towards the ending which stretches across the six days in which the heavens and the earth were created, that activity is known as reflection(فكر).

3. When inward look (نَّظَرَ))conjugates between visions of the beginning (badi, bidayah بَدِيع)and visions of the ending (عَاقِبَة) this is known as excellence (إِحْسَان). Excellence is the midmost station combining between visions of the beginning and that of the ending.

This midmost position gives us the advantage of looking back to the beginning before the six days of creation and this helps us remember God and remember ourselves. In other words we see our own beginning and this witnessing helps us to find tranquility and stillness in our heart:

"Those who believe and their hearts find tranquility through the remembrance of Allah indeed it is only through the remembrance of Allah that hearts find tranquility" Surah Ar Ra'ad [The Thunder] (13:28).

It also gives us the advantage of looking forward towards the ending (عَاقِبَة) in doing which, we are engaged in reflection (فكر). It is reflection and meditation on what may come at the end which entails various possibilities. God says:

"Know that the life of this world is nothing but sport in the day and idleness in the night and adornment and mutual vaunting amongst you and competition in amassing the wealth and the children. [the life of this world] is like a rain the growth of which is admirable to the disbelieving farmers, then it increases in growth and you see it turning yellow then it becomes chaff and in the hereafter [there is] a formidable punishment and also a forgiveness from Allah and Rizwan [Allah's good pleasure] and the life of this world is nothing but the enjoyment of delusion". Surah Al Hadid [The iron] (57:20)

The vision of multiple possibilities at the end sparks fear in the heart of the one reflecting (فكر) but also hope(طَمع). This dual reaction causes the heart to contract from fear(خَوْف) and then expand from hope.

This contraction from fear followed by expansion from hope brings the heart finally to a just middle at which point remembrance (ذِكْر) kicks in. Here we see the interdependence between the reflection(فكر) and remembrance(ذِكْر), namely reflection (فكر) if carried out to its conclusion leads up to the remembrance(ذِكْر).

Reflection as we have seen always entails duality like heaven and earth, east and west etc. for which reason reflection as a process cannot include God because God has no pair but it does lead to remembrance (ذِكْر) which applies directly to God. Reflection (فكر) is therefore an indirect way of relating to God while remembrance (ذِكْر) is immediate.

In many Quranic verses reflection and remembrance are mentioned together in the order of end first and then means or the universal first and then particular or the absolute before the relative. This is a rule we must keep in mind before approaching the Book of God for study. We must consider the whole before the parts on the principle of:

"Guide us to the way the most upright" Surah Fatihah [The Opening] (1:5)

Means worshipping is the end and seeking help is the means, He therefore put the end before the means, or the universal before the particular or the absolute before the relative. In the tradition it is narrated that prophet Muhammad peace be upon him said:

"O Allah help me to remember you, to offer gratitude to you and worship you with excellence".

Therefore remembrance, gratitude and excellence are the ends and the means are God's help otherwise it is not possible for any mortal to truly remember God or truly offer gratitude to Him or truly worship Him with excellence except through His help. Therefore God is both the end and the mean since nothing can suffice to be a means to Him.

However in terms of order and sequence the end must precede the means, the universal must precede the particular and the absolute must precede the relative. This is true because those means are created for the sake of the ends. Hence whenever God presents to us the two, He always put the end first before the means or the absolute before the relative or the universal before the particular; in order to acquaint us first with the ends before the means so that our love for the means cannot subsequently supersede our love for the end. That we know that the end exists for its own sake while the means exists for the sake of the end.

In this way, we never lose sight of the end due to our preoccupation with means, which does happen quite often to many who are seeking the truth. The means to the end become an end in itself and the true end is lost out of sight. It is due to this reason that God brings the end to our attention first before the means; so that our view of the end is not obstructed due to the interference of the means. This means that the means should be as transparent and as simple as it could be so that the end could be easily perceived through it with a full view concealing nothing about the end.

In this capacity the means is like a veil for the end; a veil which is very transparent allowing the onlookers to have a full view of the beauty of the reality that lies behind it. In other words the means act like a mirror thoroughly polished and smooth which faithfully reflect the image of the Original Truth.

In this manner all humankind is created from a male and a female however the most excellent among them is the one who most excellently reflect the excellent qualities of his Creator. Thus prophet Muhammad peace be upon him said:

"I have been sent to perfect excellent characters"

FIRST IS FIRST

Once we have attained to remembrance through the process of reflection, the sight of our heart turns towards the first creation which is the creation of the beginning:

"Say travel in the earth and see how creation began".

This first creation is known as the first fitrah:

"You indeed do know the first creation why then do you not remember?" Surah Waq'ah [The Inevitable Event] (56:62).

It is remembrance that helps one who has remembered to return back to the beginning and witness the first creation. Only the true rememberers do return back to the beginning.
Once you have known, you have indeed witnessed; for knowing is witnessing. Hence only those who have returned back to the beginning can witness. They are people of knowing (أُولُو الْعِلْمِ):

"Allah has witnessed that indeed there is no deity save He and the angels and people of the knowledge [have also witnessed] standing in uprightness. There is no deity save He, The All Mighty, The All Wise" Surah Al' Imran [The Family of Imran] (3:18).

This witnessing took place at the beginning in the first day which is the day when the Throne (عَرْش) was on water before the creation of earth and the heavens within the six days.

"And He it is who created the heavens and the earth in six days and His thrown was on water [before that] so as to try you to see who among you is excellent in action. And if you were to say to them that you indeed are going to be raised after death surely those who disbelieve will say "this is nothing but manifest sorcery" Surah Hud [Hud] (11:7).

This verse mentions about the two periods.

1. First creation
2. New creation

The period of the new creation covers the six days of creation; while the first period refers to the first creation when the Throne of God (عَرْش) was on water and that was the time before the six days of creation. The verse therefore points out that in order to attain excellence he/she must live in harmony between the two creations; the old and the new creations, without neglecting one or the other.

After the servant has got a view of the beginning and witnessed how the creation started, he is then transported to the ending to take another view of the ending and witness how creation will take place. God says:

"Were we ever worned out by the first creation? Nay! They now are in confusion about a new creation" Surah Qaf [Qaf] (50:15).

"Say "Travel in the earth and look at how He started the creation. Then Allah will raise the last creation". Verily Allah has power over everything" Surah Ankaboot [The Spider] (29:20).

In this way God's servant combines between witnessing of the beginning and witnessing of the ending.

God says:

"Verily in the creation of the heavens and of the earth and in the alternation of the night and of the day are surely signs for people of the heart"

"Those who remember Allah standing and sitting and on their sides and they reflect on the creation of the heavens and of the earth [and they say] O our Lord! You have not created all this in vain. Glory be unto you so protect us from the punishment of the fire" Surah Al' Imran [The Family of Imran] (3:190-191).

These verses as we see refer to both remembrance (ذِكْر) and then to reflection (فكر) on the principle of end before the means. In the first verse (190) we are presented with the four signs heaven, earth, night, and day. Once the signs are identified the next step is to ponder and reflect on the creation of these signs which means to ponder about how they were created. Once we started to ponder about how they were created this will take us farther back to determine of what substances they were made of. Then we find the original pair to come to remembrance.
Remembrance is divided into three categories:
1. To remember God standing
2. To remember God sitting
3. To remember God reclining
The first remembrance in the standing position is the remembrance of witnessing:

"And if you fear a breach between the two of them, then appoint an umpire from his folk and an umpire from her folk. If they two truly intend reconciliation then Allah will reconcile between the two of them. Verily Allah is all knowing all acquainted" Surah An Nisa [The Women] (4:35)

"O you who believe! Be those who stand for Allah witnesses to the uprightness and let not the hatred of people incite you to evildoing that you do not act in justice. Act justly that is nearer to Allah's reverence and revere Allah. Verily Allah is all acquainted about all that you do" Surah Al Maidah [The Table Spread] (5:8).

The second remembrance is the remembrance through glorification while third is the remembrance through supplication.
In another verse God says:

"Say "I only invite you to do one thing to stand for Allah in pairs and singles and then reflect" There is no madness in your companion. He is but a warner for you ahead of a formidable punishment" Surah Saba [The City Of Saba] (34:46).

In this verse first we are urged to stand in odds or in pairs as we remember Allah and then we ponder within ourselves which will lead us to ponder on the creations of the heaven and the earth and which eventually will lead us to reflect upon the end of time and the coming of the hour then we will truly realize that Muhammad peace be upon him was indeed a warner about that coming doom.

LOWERING THE GAZE

God the Almighty has created two lives: one is the outer life of the outer world and the other is the inner life of the inner world.
The outer life of the outer world is commonly known as the life of this world (دُنْيَا) while the inner life of the inner world is called as life of hereafter (الْآخِرَة). Each world has been adorned with its appropriate adornments. These adornments like any adornments are meant to attract attention unto the wearer. Thus the adornment of the inner world attracts attention of the seeker towards the inner world likewise attraction of the outer world draws attention to the outer life. God says:

"And verily We are going to reduce everything on it to a sand of rubbles"

Or do you count that the companions of the cave and of the wall to be a marvel among our signs" Surah Kahf [The Cave] (18:8-9).

"The wealth and the children are adornment of the life of this world. But the things that are righteous and sustaining are better in reward in the sight of your Lord and are better in hope" Surah Kahf [The Cave] (18:46).

Thus everything that this outer world is adorned with, including wealth and children all incite towards the love of this outer life all of which, after all, will come to an end.
On the other hand all that the inner world is adorned with which is similar to the adornment of the outer world are all designed to attract people towards the love of inner life which is everlasting because it is linked to the love of God which is ever living with no beginning and no ending. God says:

"We truly believe in our Lord hoping that He will forgive us our faults and all that magic that you have compelled us to and Allah is best and lasting" Surah Taha [Taha] (20:73).

The inner life which lasts forever is associated with God and the outer life which is temporary is not, hence we are commanded by God to lower our gaze from the adornments of the outer world so that we are not enticed by the outer life unto the adornments of the inner world, so that we are attracted towards the inner life. This is the universal meaning of lowering the gaze rather than the particular meaning. God says in the Quran:

"Tell Tell the believers to lower part of their gaze and to safeguard their chastity. That is purer for them. Verily Allah is well acquainted with all that they manufacture" Surah An Nur [The Light] (24:30).

The word Farj_furjaha(فَرْجَهَا __ فَرْج) means a piece of flesh which on the basis of principle that the universal comes before the particular we can say that it refers to the heart universally and the human anatomy in particular. As one who safeguards his heart had no hardship saving his/her chastity while the one who safeguards his/her chastity might be unable to safeguard his heart, wherein reverence (تَقْوَى) truly lies. God says:

"So it is that whoever reveres the insignia of Allah that truly comes from the reverence of Allah that is in the hearts" Surah Al-Hajj [The Pilgrimage] (22:32)

In a prophetic tradition Prophet Muhammad peace be upon him is reported to have said:

'Taqwa is indeed here' pointing to his heart three times; which means that the true safeguarding is the safeguarding of the heart.

This is true because the treasure of faith (إِيمَن) lies in the heart. It is that treasure that must be safeguarded against the thieves and the highway robbers who day by day wait for the believer in order to rob him of the treasure in his heart.

Whenever God invites us to lower our gaze in fact he asks us to have a look within our own hearts and behold that treasure of faith that lies at the core of our own hearts. This treasure however, is adorned on one hand and protected on the other. In a similar manner, God placed stars in the heaven for ornamentation and protection.

Similarly when we lower our gaze and look within our hearts we find that our hearts are like doorways that open on to the entire inner world. The first thing that we notice is stars that God has placed on the threshold on the inner world to invite the believers in and to repel those who disbelieve. What we have been used to seeing outwardly like the stars, the moon, the sun we now see them from inside their reality and originality; we now see everything from within, (مَلَكُوت) and our perception changes completely in that we see things from inside out rather than outside in. In this way we look at the universal value in them before the particular.

Even though both the inner and outer values are taken into consideration however what is seen first always prevails over the second one. Therefore one who sees the outer first before the inner, the outer will prevail over the inner in the end. On the contrary one who sees the inner first before the outer, the inner at the end will prevail.

An example of that is the story of Abraham and his people in which he broke their idols and left the axe hanging on the biggest idol which was the sole remnant. When they questioned him regarding the broken idols he replied, ask the big one, may be the big one did it because he is the only remaining idol.

For a moment his words awakened them and they turned back to their hearts and then admitted that he was right and that they had done wrong to themselves by worshipping idols that can neither speak nor benefit nor harm them. No sooner did they make their confession that they relapse back to their former state, defending their idols and condemning Ibrahim: their awakener. God says:

When he said to his father and his people "What are these images to which you are so avowedly devoted"

When he said to his father and his people "What are these images to which you are so avowedly devoted"

They said "We found our fathers worshipping them"

He said "then you and your fathers were indeed in a manifest error"

They said "Have you come to us with the truth or are you one of those who sport"

He said "Nay your Lord is the Lord of the heavens and of the earth who initiated their creation and I am among the witnesses to that"

"and by Allah I will most certainly discomfit your idols with my scheme after you turn your backs away"

So he broke them into pieces except the biggest of them so that they might return to it

They said "Who has done this to our gods. He indeed is of those who are wrongful"

They said "We heard a young man called Abraham speak ill of them"

They said "Then bring him under the eyes of the people perhaps they will witness"

They said "Is it you who did this to our gods O Abraham?"

He said "Nay it was done by this the biggest one among them ask them if they can speak"

So they returned back to their own souls therefore they said "Verily you yourself are doing wrong to your own souls"

Then they reverted back to their former position [and said] "You know indeed that these cannot speak"

He said "Do you then worship besides Allah something that can neither benefit you in aught nor can it harm you

"Fie on you and on those that you worship besides Allah. Do you have no understanding"

They said "Burn him and give victory to your gods if you are going to do something"

We said "O fire be cool and peace upon Abraham"" Surah Al Anbiyaa [The Prophets] (21:52-69).

This is the case of people whose view of outer life prevails over the life of inner world. Their eyes are awake to outer life and their hearts are sleeping to the life of inner world. If someone arouses them from their slumber and gives them a momentary awakening to the inner life with its beauty and majesty they experience a moment of excitement and fervour. However as soon as that excitement subsides they revert back to their former condition of outer awakening and inner slumber. This perennial state of slumber in the heart punctuated by sporadic awakening is described in Quran.

"Their example is like the example of one who lit off a fire but when it brightened all that was around him, Allah took away their light and left them in darknesses so they do not see"

"Deaf and dumb and blind so that they do not return"

"or like a cloud storm from the sky in it there are darknesses and thunder and lightning. They put their fingers in their ears from the thunderstruck for fear of the death. For Allah is all encompassing around the disbelievers"

"The lightning almost snatches away their sights. Whenever He makes it bright for them, they walk in it [in the brightness] but when He turns it dark on them, they stand still. And had Allah so pleased, He would have surely taken away their hearing and their sights. Verily Allah has power over everything" Surah Al Baqarah [The Cow] (2:17-20)

They move by leaps and bounds caused by a momentary glow of a body of light. As long as that body of glow lasts they move on, when it passes away they stop moving; as they have no light to move by since they possess no inner light to fall back on when the outer glow passes away.
One who has a true awakening of the heart always has a residue of light which is perpetually enhanced from within so that each time the exciting glow of the outer light passes away and the darkness sets in, he/she takes resource to inner light which is within his heart. This is the contrast between the glamour of the outer world and the true beauty of the inner life.
When the Arabs of the desert said to the Prophet Muhammad peace be upon him we have faith; God said to him tell them you have no faith, because faith has not yet penetrated into your heart:

"The desert Arabs said "We believe" Say "You have not believed [in truth] but you just say 'We have submitted ourselves' but the faith has not yet entered into your hearts" and if you obey Allah and His messenger, He will not cheat you of anything from your deeds. Verily Allah is Oft-Forgiving Most Merciful" Surah Al Hujraat [The Inner Apartments] (49:14).

Therefore God makes distinction between who looks at faith from within his heart. The source and support for his faith come from within so that the existence of his faith does not depend on outwardly. It is constant and ever-growing.

On the contrary a person whose faith is dependent on outward life and its temporary glamor; his faith does not have steadiness and continuity simply because the outward life is constantly changing from state to state from high to low. In a similar manner the faith which is invested on outer life is subject to having moments of elevation and elation quickly succeeded by other moments of fall and shrinking. These actual experiences from one extreme to the other are unknown to those whose faith is internalized and draw their substance from inner life which is everlasting. God says:

"What you have will finish and what is with Allah is lasting and certainly We will reward those who are patient with the reward of the best that they ever did" Surah An Nahl [The Bee] (16:96).

This contrast between the two kinds of faith outer and inner is again beautifully presented to us through the story of Prophet Abraham and his people. As he tried to make his people understand that faith does not depend on things that are seen from outside in the outward life; rather faith is a reality that lies within the heart because only then this faith continues to prosper forever unlike the faith supported by outer life which is subject to vicissitudes of outer life.

To reach this simple truth he saw a star at night, he exclaimed "here is my Lord", when the star set he remarked: "I do not like things that set". Then came the moon and he said the same. Finally came the sun and he said the same. He hoped that they understand that if any one invests his faith in a star, his faith will last as long as its rising; as soon as star falls his faith too falls with it, the same goes for the moon and for the sun.

The only thing that in which you will invest your faith will continue to be steady and never fluctuate with, is God. Once your heart is awakened by faith in God your heart will never sleep again so as well once your heart is connected to the inner life your heart will never die again. It is eternal life and eternal awakening.
This story is mentioned in Quran:

"and when Abraham said to his father Azar "Do you take idols for gods? Verily I see you and your people in a misguidance most evident"

and thus We show Abraham the inner kingdom of the heavens and of the earth and so that he may become of those who have attained to certitude

So when the night engulfed him, he saw a star. He exclaimed "This is my Lord" But when it set, he said "I love not the things that set"

Then when he saw the moon appearing in glory, he exclaimed "This is my Lord" But when it set, he said "If my Lord does not guide me, surely I will be of the people who have gone astray

But then when he saw the sun rising in glory, he exclaimed "This is my Lord; this is the most great" but when it set, he said "O my people! I indeed disavow all that you ascribe as partners to Him

I indeed, have set my face to the One who originated the heavens and the earth, in sincere devotion and I am not of those who ascribe partners to Him" Surah Al An'am [The Cattle] (6:74-79).

Despite the increasing efforts by prophets' and their successors to change peoples' perception from looking outward to looking inward, most human beings have remained stiff to these attempts thus God says in consolation to prophet Muhammad peace be upon him:

"And most people will not be believers despite your ardent desire" Surah Yusuf [Joseph] (12:103).

Most people are therefore not believers even though they seem to be one. They perform rituals of religion and they fulfil their various duties; still God says that most of them are not believers because their hearts are not awakened to the inner life.
As for most of the believers the source of their faith is outwardly not inwardly therefore sometimes they believe and sometimes they don't; sometimes their faith is in high, sometimes in low.

Furthermore we are told by God that most of those who believe in Him do so but ascribe partners to Him as described in verse 106 of chapter Yusuf. This verse completes the meaning of verse 103 of chapter Yusuf that most people are not believers. Believers here mean true believers.

"And most of them do not believe in Allah without ascribing partners to Him" Surah Yusuf [Joseph] (12:106)

True believers according to verse 106 are those who believe in God with total self-surrender (tasleem تسليم). Faith when joined with self-surrender becomes pure faith. God says:

"Those who have faith and have not admixed their belief with any wrong, it is they for whom there is the safety while it is they who are well guided" Surah Al An'am [The Cattle] (6:82)

In order for faith to remain pure it must be based on self-surrender (تسليم). Faith (إيمَن) is the substance and self-surrender (تسليم) is the refinery. If the substance of faith passes through the refinery of self-submission it comes out pure and immaculate. If the substance of faith is not passed through the refinery of self-surrender it comes out mixed and adulterated. God says:

"And when the believers saw the confederates they said "This is what Allah and His messenger promised us and Allah and His messenger have said the truth" and this did not increase them in anything except belief and self-submission" Surah Al Ahzab [The Confederates] (33:22).

At another place God says:

"But nay by your Lord, they will not truly believe until they make you an arbitrator in all the matters that arise between them and thereafter they will not feel any constriction within themselves because of the decision you made and they will submit a complete submission" Surah An Nisa [The Women] (4:65).

TWIN SISTERS

The word 'sign' (ءَايَةٌ) is feminine in Arabic so that when God speaks of His signs as being in pairs He refers to them as sisters. God says in Quran:

"And We didn't show them a sign except that it was greater than its sister and We seized them with the punishment so that perhaps they may return" Surah Zukhraf [The Gold Adornments] (43:48).

In a prophetic tradition it is also narrated that Prophet Muhammad peace be upon him said:

"Hud and its sister has turned my hair grey".

The sisterhood here is between one chapter of Quran to another (surah) while in the formerly quoted verse it is between a sign and another or between one verse and another. The point which is stressed here is that every sign has a sister sign, every verse has a sister verse and every chapter has a sister chapter. So that when we find one sign we should look for the sister sign and when we find one verse we must look for her sister and the same goes for one chapter to another. If we draw a conclusion based on one without the other our conclusion will be impartial and imbalanced.

SUN AND MOON

Among the signs which are paired as sisters is sun and moon. God says in Quran:

"And among His signs are the night and the day and the sun and the moon. Do not prostrate to the sun nor to the moon but prostrate to Allah the one who created them if it is indeed Him that you worship" Surah Fussilat [Expounded] (41:37).

God called the sun the big sign "Ayah Kabira" and the moon as small "Aya Saghira". The terms big (kabir) and small (saghir) do not merely put emphasis on the size of one or the other but rather on the nature of the particles of which it is composed. The particles of the sun are known as "kbr" (كِبْر) and the particles of the moon are known as "sighr (صغر)". These particles behave in different ways. The particles of the sun (kibr__كِبْر) are hot and ascending and while the particles of the moon are cool and descending.
Sun is hot and ascending while moon is cool and descending. Union between the kibr of the sun and sghr of the moon gives complete cycle

"And the sun and the moon are made into one" Surah Al Qiyamah [The Resurrection] (75:9)

In order to reach a full cycle and fulfill the word of God the particles of sun and the particles of the moon must be kept in their due proportions without excess or recess.

"It is not fitting for the sun to overtake the moon nor for the night to advance the day. And each swimming in an orbit" Surah Ya-sin [Ya-sin] (36:40)

Where the cycle is complete and the word fulfilled, thence begins true remembrance (ذِكْر).

"And from everything We have created pairs so that you may remember [the one who has no pair]" Surah Adh Dhariyat [The Winds That Scatter] (51:49)

Meaning that whenever a pair is united in harmony and balance without excess of one over the other, the word of God is fulfilled thereby and the cycle is completed. Only then does true remembrance of God begins and through remembrance of God hearts find complete tranquility.

DAY AND NIGHT

Day and night also form a pair. The relationship between them differs from the relationship between the sun and the moon. It is not a relationship of big to small rather fast to slow nor between ascending and descending but rather between translucency and opacity, nor between hot and cool rather between resonance and silence. The particles of the day are known as kunnas (كُنَّس). Their characteristics are: swiftness, translucence and resonance. On the other hand the particles of night known as "Khunnas" (خُنَّس) are characteristically slow, opaque and silent. God says in Quran:

"So I do swear by the Khunnas [heavy and slow moving night particles]

"And by the flowing Kunnas [light and fast moving day particles]" Surah At Takwir [The Roll Up] (81:15-16)

When the kunnas of the day and the khunnas of the night are united in their due proportions a well-balanced middle state is attained whereby the individual's pace is neither fast nor slow, his voice neither loud nor silent, neither overactive nor over passive. True remembrance is born out of this well balanced state. God says:

Say "call Allah or call Ar-Rahman by whichever name you call him all the excellent names are His. And do not read your prayer aloud nor make it silent and find a way between them [neither loud nor silent]" Surah Al Isra [The Night Journey] (17:110)

With regards to one's pace God says:

"And take a mid-course in your walk and lower from your voice. Verily the most detestable of all sounds in the braying of the donkeys" Surah Luqman [Luqman] (31:19)

Also God says:

"And We have made the night and the day as two signs. We have darkened the sign of the night and We have made the sign of the day bright so that you may seek a favor from your Lord and so that you may know the number of years and computation and everything have We detailed with complete detailing _"Surah Al Isra [The Night Journey] (17:12)

meaning that God has divided the night and the day into pairs of signs. He caused the particles of the night (خُنَّس) to be invisible (مَحَوْنَا) meaning opaque and compact so that like a thick black veil that whatever lies behind becomes partly or fully invisible. On the other hand He caused the particles of the day (كُنَّس) to be visible (مُبْصِرَة) which means that they are transparent, light and spaced so that like an extremely fine and thin veil they fully reveal whatever lies behind them.
In this way sunlight is revealed in all its glory through the extremely fine and transparent particles of the day. The primary function of the day is to vehiculate the sunlight but still withhold its full brunt. For as fine as the kunnas are, they still reduce the full impact of the sunlight for unless the kunnas interpose between the earth and the sunlight, it surely will burn down everything on the earth:

"By the sun and its brilliance

"And by the moon as she follows it"

"And by the day as it makes manifest it's [Sun's] brilliance"

"And by the night as it covers it" Surah Ash Shams [The Sun] (91:1-4)

The khunasses are however ill-suited to transmit the hot and elevated solar particles because of their distance and also because the kunasses interpose between the sun on one hand and between the moon and the night particles on the other hand.
The khunasses are however better suited to vehiculate the moonlight because of the various concordances between the two. Because the moonlight is cool and descending the khunasses are able to keep with the speed allowing for its slow and cool light to seep through gently and slowly in the manner of flowing water.
In the end we have two types of cycles:
a) Which is lunar
b) Which is solar
The motion in lunar cycle is punctuated by pauses therefore slow,

"And the moon We have measured for it phases until it comes back like the old crooked data stalk" Surah Yasin [Yasin] (36:39)

This type of fractionary motion by moon has given rise to calculation by fractions (حِسَاب).

On the other hand the straight forward motion of the sun (جَرَىْ) has taught man the knowledge of numbers ('adad).

"It is He who caused the sun to be a blazing light and the moon to be a cool light and who apportioned for it stations so that you may know the number of years and computation. Allah did not create that except by the truth. He details the signs for a people who know" Surah Yunus [Jonah] (10:5)

Therefore numbering (عَدَد) belongs to the solar cycle and while calculation (حِسَاب) belongs to the domain of lunar cycles.

However beyond all these we seek the favour (fadl فضل) of Allah which cannot be numbered or calculated. God says:

"And since you have disassociated yourself from them and all that they worship other than Allah therefore retire yourself to the cave and your Lord will spread out for you from His mercy and will prepare for you ease out of your affair " Surah Al Kahf [The Cave] (18:16)

God's favours are wholes (عَدَد) and numbering applies only to whole while calculation (حِسَاب)applies to parts and fragments.

THE SPIRIT AND THE SOUL

The relationship between the spirit and the soul as a pair is exactly the same as the one between the sun and the moon alternately our life is under the influence of one or the other. When it is the reign of the spirit (رُوح) our life is coursing through a period of full daylight with all its abundant qualities like wakefulness, clarity of vision etc. All along during this period we see things only as whole in total oblivion to parts and fragments. In turn when our life comes under the reign of the soul it takes us on a night journey where stillness and inactivity are the norm.

In the best case each of the two spirit and soul are required to play their respective roles by turns without one encroaching on the other so that we can live a life which is harmonious and well balanced. God says:

"It is not fitting for the sun to overtake the moon nor for the night to advance the day. And each swimming in an orbit " Surah Ya-sin [Ya-sin] (36:40)

The spirit therefore, must not override the soul to the point of wiping out its existence, but the night which is the vehicle for the soul must not advance the day which is the vehicle for the spirit. In the event where our spirit overtakes our soul, our entire life will turn into a day without a night which means that our entire life is dominated by the kunnasses which keep us awake and active continuously. If however our soul pre-empts our sprit our entire life will turn into a night without day whereby it is dominated entirely by the khunnasses which keep us still and inactive. As a result our life will be either one of extreme wakefulness and activity or extreme dullness and inactivity. God says:
"***Say "See if Allah were to make the night to last on you forever till the day of resurrection which deity other than Allah will bring you brightness. Will you not then hear?"***

Say "See if Allah were to make the day to last on your forever till the day of resurrection, which deity other than Allah will bring you a night wherein you can rest. Will you not then see?"

"And out of His mercy, He has made the night and the day for you so that you may find rest in it and that you may seek from his favor and perhaps that you may be grateful"

" Surah Al Qasas [The Narrations] (71-73).

The objective behind the alternation of the day and the night is to regulate our life between rest and pursuit so that we may eventually attain the station of gratitude (شُكْر)through which we can earn God's pleasure (رِضْوَان).

In other words our life must be regulated between the spirit (رُوح) which brings wakefulness and activity to our life and the soul which gives stillness and rest to our life too. In this manner we can attain to remembrance (ذِكْر) and gratitude (شُكْر) and from gratitude leads to God's pleasure (رِضْوَان). God says:

"And it is He who has made the night and the day to alternate for such a one who seeks to remember Allah or seeks to offer gratitude" Surah Al Furqan [The Criterion] (25:62).

Regulation between the spirit and soul brings about remembrance. Remembrance triggers off gratitude and gratitude leads to God's pleasure (رِضْوَان).

Remembrance (ذِكْر) as we have seen always develops from the harmonious conjugation of a pair; be that the spirit and the soul or the sun and the moon or the day and the night or the kunnas and the khunnas or the east and the west or the heavens and the earth and so on. God says:

"And from everything We have created pairs so that you may remember [the one who has no pair]" Surah Adh Dhariyat [The Winds That Scatter] (51:49)

Remembrance therefore is the fruit of unification between two principles. This effort of unification (Jam'a____جَمْع) between two principles is known as fikr normally translated as reflection. It means the ability to unite between two principles by force of meditation. Through the force of meditation we pull together two principles:

1. Which encapsulates the energy substance
2. The other which explodes that hidden energy substance in the former and turns it into an active energy substance.

The whole process is known as ignition (talqeeh_ تلقيح); the first one is the ignited one and the second one is igniter. God says:

"And We sent the winds which are rousers [for the clouds] so We sent down from the heaven water and so We caused you to drink from it but you are not the one charged for being treasurers for it" Surah Al Hijr [The Rocky Tract] (15:22).

The word winds here refers to the two categories of winds one that contains the energy substance and the other that contains the igniting principle; when the two successfully meet so that the energy substance in one is exploded by the other, light is produced bright as lightning and life also is produced in the form of rain water. God says:

"Have you not seen that Allah draws a cloud then He puts it together then He reduces it into a pile and then you see the rain coming out from between it and He sends down from the heaven from mountains therein from hail with which He strikes whom He pleases and averts from whom He pleases. The brilliance of its lightning almost nearly snatches away the sights" Surah An Nur [The Light] (24:43)

Hence as shown in this verse the imbrication between the clouds that contain the energy substance and the one which contains the igniter produce both rain for life on the one hand and light on the other hand for guidance and many other verses to this purpose are mentioned in the Quran in the following verses:

"and He it is who sends the winds as bringers of glad tidings ahead of His mercy until when it has lifted up a heavy laden cloud, We drive it onto a dead land and We send down the water thereat and We cause all kinds of produce to come forth thereby. Thus do We bring forth the dead so that you may remember"

"As for the good land, its produce comes out by the leave of its Lord and as for the one which is bad, it does not come out except meagrely. Thus do We present the signs in multiple forms for a people who offer gratitude" Surah Al A'raaf [The Heights] (7:57-58).

At another place God says:

"And Allah it is He who sends the wind so that they raise a cloud, then We draw it to a dead land and We cause the earth to come to life by it after its death. Thus will be resurrection" Surah Al Fatir [The Originator] (35:9).

Also God says:

"Allah it is He who sends the wind so that it raises a cloud and then He spreads it in the sky the way He pleases and then He reduces it into pieces and then you see the rain drop issuing forth from within it and if He brings it onto any whom He pleases from among His servants lo! they are rejoicing

Even though before it was sent down on them, they truly were in despair before it

So look at the effects of the mercy of Allah how He brings the earth to life after its death. Verily He is the one who is going to bring the dead to life and it is He who has power over everything

And if We send a wind and they see it turn yellow they will continue to disbelieve after it" Surah Ar Rum [The Romans] (30:48-51).

"Have you not seen that Allah draws a cloud then He puts it together then He reduces it into a pile and then you see the rain coming out from between it and He sends down from the heaven from mountains therein from hail with which He strikes whom He pleases and averts from whom He pleases. The brilliance of its lightning almost nearly snatches away the sights" Surah Al Furqan [The Criterion] (24:43)

All these verses expound on the method by which God produces life and light out of the two fundamental principles of existence: the principle that nourishes the energy substance and the one that ignites it.
As we read these verses which relate to the generation of life and light through the interaction between the two principles, we notice the recurrence of certain words like "Rkm (ركاما)" a pile, "Ksf (كِسَف)" debris which refer to the particles kunnas and khunnas which are the igniting and the conceiver principles respectively. Another important term that occurs in these verses is "Athara أثرا" (فَتُثِيرُ) which means rouse. The winds play the role of inciters or catalysts; in other words they rouse the clouds which carry the principles and drive them against one another towards a destination they must meet therein. This causes a fierce race between the clouds that carry the kunnas and those carrying the khunnas each wanting to outrun the other. Their speed depends on the degree and nature of the rousing.
In terms of nature we mean wind which is the carrier, which may be carrier of glad tidings (بُشْرَىٰ) or carrier of warnings (نُذُور). The carrier of glad tidings contains khunnas and the carrier of warning contains kunnas.
In terms of degree we mean the intensity of the rousing (Atherat). If the rousing is stronger the particles move faster and if the rousing is weaker the particles move slower. In this case the khunnas may outrun the kunnas although the latter by nature are swifter and lighter; but if the rousing is weak the khunnas may out run them.
Another reason for khunnas to outrun the kunnas is when the khunnas are roused before the kunnas thus having lead over the kunnas. God says:

"Your Lord indeed is Allah, Who created the heavens and the earth in six periods, then He established His presence over the throne. He causes the night to cover the day following it in swift pursuit and (He created) the sun and the moon, and the stars subservient through His commandment. Lo! for Him is the creation and the commandment. Blessed is Allah Lord of the worlds" Surah Al A'raaf [The Heights] (7:54)

The issue of the race is judged in favour of the winner. If the kunnas reaches first than it is ranked higher but if the khunnas reaches first then it is ranked supreme. Hence the meaning of the verse:

"He makes the night to enter into the day and the day to enter into the night and He has made the sun and the moon subservient [through His command] each running to an appointed term. That is Allah your lord for Him is the dominion and those that you call besides Him do not possess as much as the skin of a date-stone" Surah Al Fatir [The Originator] (35:13).

"You cause the night to enter into the day and You cause the day to enter into the night and You bring the living forth from the dead and You bring the dead forth from the living and You provide whom You please without calculation"Surah Al Imran [The Family of Imran] (3:27).

The fierce race between the kunnas and khunnas each trying to outstrip the other is beautifully presented in Quran through the analogy of thorough bred chargers as their riders press them eagerly towards the battle field where they join the melee. God says:

"By the gallopers with resounding breasts

And by those who enkindle sparkles of fire

And by the raiders in the morning

And by the raiders in the morning

And they make their encounter in the midst thereof" Surah Al A'diyaat [The Swift Runners] (100:1-5).

This beautiful description of the horses racing towards the battlefield is a metaphor for the particles of kunnas (the day particles) as they spread at dawn racing out and vying with one another to catch up with the khunnas(night particles) as they recede back with the night. Their major characteristics (the kunnas) are out lined in the following words:

1. They gallop (عَٰدِيَٰت):

This refers to their ability to spring up and move fast. The word (dbh__(ضَبْح).) translated as panting and snorting refers to their extreme sharpness which cuts through the throat of the enemies(dbh__slaughter), it also refers to the loud concussion that erupts out of their friction with one another.

2. They strike sparks of fire (فَالْمُورِيَاتِ قَدْحًا):

Refer to the sparks of fire that comes off from their collision with one another. These sparks of fire are like blinding radiance of lightning. Also God says:

"Have you not seen that Allah draws a cloud then He puts it together then He reduces it into a pile and then you see the rain coming out from between it and He sends down from the heaven from mountains therein from hail with which He strikes whom He pleases and averts from whom He pleases. The brilliance of its lightning almost nearly snatches away the sights" Surah Al Noor [The Light] (24:43)

3. They make raids at dawn (فَالْمُغِيرَاتِ صُبْحًا):

This refers to both the manner in which they charge at their targets and the time they make their raid. As for the manner the term "raid" informs us about the swiftness with which they swoop down at their target as well as the terror they strike in the hearts of their enemies; as they take them by surprise. It also cuts image for us, the image of an avid pursuer chasing diligently after its prey. As for the time it's the dawn time when the kunnas begin to spread out in quest of finding their mates.

4. They spread there at clouds of dust (فَأَثَرْنَ بِهِ نَقْعًا) which they raise in their wake. This cloud of dust is produced as they rub against one another producing debris which accumulate and heap up into a cloud of dust.

5. They penetrate their midst at dawn (فَوَسَطْنَ بِهِ جَمْعًا) in the midst thereof:

This refers to the kunnas reaching at dawn their final station which is neither easterly nor westerly. It is at this point that life and light are manifested. God says:

"Allah is the light of the heavens and of the earth. Likeness of His light is like a niche within which is a lamp and the lamp is within a glass and the glass looks like a brilliant star lit from a blessed olive tree that is neither in the east nor in the west. Its oil almost nearly illuminates even though fire has not touched it. It is a light upon a light. Allah guides unto His light whom He pleases and Allah sets forth the parables for the mankind and Allah is all knowing about everything" Surah Al Noor [The Light] (24:35)

THE EXPLOSION OF STARS

Know that the description given above about the particles of kunnas and how they spread out at dawn driven by God's design to their appointed destination come all but a result of the explosion of stars which takes place during the last third of the night little before dawn. The explosion of stars is due to their expansion as a result of the impact of Divine commandment pronounced by Almighty God. As they bow their heads down and fall prostrate in front of the Divine verdict they experience their greatest expansion which causes them to explode into millions of particles known as essences_ zawaat. As a result one star has developed into million others this is the manner in which God makes the universe grow and expand. However, growth and expansion is available to such being as willingly surrender to will of God, bowing and prostrating in the face of His commandment. God says:

"And the star and the tree are in prostration" Surah Ar Rahman [The Most Gracious] (55:6).

At another place God says:

"Lo! I swear by the setting of the stars" Surah Al Waqi'ah [The Inevitable Event] (56:75).

"By the star when it falls" Surah An Najam [The Star] (53:1).

In the chapter Al Noor of Quran God makes the light of stars and the light of fire joined together as a parable for His light; in the aya e noor(verse of light).
God says:

"Allah is the light of the heavens and of the earth. Likeness of His light is like a niche within which is a lamp and the lamp is within a glass and the glass looks like a brilliant star lit from a blessed olive tree that is neither in the east nor in the west. Its oil almost nearly illuminates even though fire has not touched it. It is a light upon a light. Allah guides unto His light whom He pleases and Allah sets forth the parables for the mankind and Allah is all knowing about everything" Surah An Noor [The Light] (24:35).

Here again star is mentioned with along with fire in reference to the phenomenon of explosion of stars into millions of particles which are ignited by fire producing light upon light.

It is narrated by Imam Al Bokhari that the prophet peace be upon him said:

"Whenever God pronounces His sentence of truth in the heaven it sounds like the noise when iron falls on a rock, thereupon all the inhabitants of the heaven fell down in prostration; angel Jibril will be the first to raise his head and as he comes down the heavens, he is asked by the company of angels: "what has our Lord decreed? "He says: "the Truth".

In this prophetic tradition we see how the prophet Muhammad peace be upon him has made reference to the prostration of stars and their explosion by terms like *"the noise made by iron as it falls on the rock".*

This is the sound produced when the stars exploded into millions of particles which they collide together producing such a sound.

In another tradition narrated by Bokhari, prophet Muhammad peace be upon him said when asked how does revelation come to you. He said: *"sometimes the angel comes to me in the form of a man he relays to me (the message) and I comprehend what he said, at other times it comes to me like ringing of a bell".*

The ringing of a bell means the particles are exploded as they forerun the Divine communication. In the first case which is when the angel comes in the form of man brings the message, the divine communication comes with glad tidings, in the second case when it comes like the ringing of a bell the Divine communication consists of warning. Hence the prophet Muhammad peace be upon him was both a warner and a bringer of glad tidings.

ATTAINING TO CERTITUDE

When God the Almighty has willed to select one of His servants and raise from creation to commandment, he first prepares Him. This preparation consists of changing the order in which his perceptions are disposed. The usual order is hearing (ears)---seeing(eyes) and comprehending(heart). This order is reversed to heart---eyes---ears so that he perceives with his heart before he witnesses with his eyes or hear with his ears. This is the order in which people are raised on the day of judgment. On that day having attained to certitude those who have failed in their earthly life ask God to send them back in order they may act righteously because now they attained to certitude. They say:

"If only you could see when the evildoers are going to bend their heads low in the presence of their Lord saying "O our Lord! We have seen and we have heard so send us back [to the earth] and we shall work righteousness for verily we now have certitude" Surah As Sajda [The Prostration] (32:12).

However certitude may not be attainable by many in this life who have to act righteously on the strength of their faith.

MOSES PEACE BE UPON HIM SEES THE FIRE

When Moses peace be upon him, left Median with his family he espied a fire. The word "ra'a" is used in Quranic text instead of "absara" which indicates that he saw the fire with his heart (رَءَا) and not with his eyes (أَبْصَرَ). Furthermore it was Moses alone who saw the fire and not his family because his heart could see what they couldn't. The coolness which he was feeling which proceeded from the light of stars cast over him, created a yearning in his heart to look for fire in order to warm himself and those with him.

The next step which Moses took was to follow his vision with action by seeking after what he was yearning for. He made the effort to go towards the fire. This also is an indication that if you are granted a vision by God, it is your turn to struggle to make it come true. Accordingly Moses made the effort and went towards the fire. As he said to his family, his purpose was to procure two things: fire to warm them up and information to guide them on their way.

According to the story the three most important steps towards the fulfilment of a vision have been taken:

1. Having a true vision
2. A firm intention to reach the objective of the vision
3. The actual outward movement towards achieving the objectives.

The first two, vision and intention take place at the level of the heart. The last one involves the use of hearing sight and limbs in order to translate the vision into reality. Accordingly Moses came unto the fire, as soon as he reached the fire it branded his heart turning the cool oil of faith in his heart into a radiant lamp spreading brightness all around. This was the firebrand he came looking for. Secondly God spoke to him and also permitted Moses to speak, imparting to him both abilities to hear, speak and see. Thus his heart, his sight, his tongue and his hearing were all expanded. Thus he also found the guidance which he came looking for, Quran says:

"When he saw a fire he said to his family "tarry here. I have indeed perceived a fire maybe I can bring you from it a brand or I can find guidance at the fire" Surah Taha [Taha] (20:10).

When Moses returned back to his family he brought back to them light and guidance he went looking for. The light and the guidance he brought back with him were incorporated in to the Torah so that those who are seeking light can be enlightened by it and those who are seeking guidance can find therein the guidance. As Quran says:

"We have indeed sent down the Torah, in it there is guidance and light. The prophets who have submitted themselves to Allah deliver judgement through it for those who adhere to Judaism and so do the Rabbis and the sages because of what they were entrusted from the book of Allah and they were witnesses over it. Therefore do not have defer to men but defer to Me and do not sell My signs for a trifling price and whoever does not judge by that which Allah has sent, then they are the ones who are the disbelievers" Surah Al Maida [The Table spread] (5:44).

Beside the light and guidance God also gave Moses signs to prove that he was coming from God. With these signs he confronted pharaoh and his magicians. The stick which he carried turned into snake and swallowed the snakes of magicians. The magicians knew that their science of magic does not extend beyond physical manipulation so when they saw the Moses' stick turned into a snake which swallowed their snakes as it had life; they instantly believed in Moses. As for Moses' hand which shined forth like a sun had the effect of removing freeze from the eyes of onlookers due to the spell cast over their eyes to prevent them from seeing reality.

MAGICIANS AND POETS

The two most formidable enemies of the truth at any time are magicians and poets. The magicians on their part play tricks on the sights of people to prevent them from looking for or perceiving truth. While the poets on their part endeavour to distract the ears of the people from listening to or hearing the truth through their eloquence:

"From among mankind are such who buy idle talk in order to misguide without any knowledge from the way of Allah and he takes it for a matter of jest. It is they for whom there is a debasing punishment" Surah Luqman [Luqman] (31:6)

Moses encounter was mainly with the first group while Prophet Muhammad peace be upon him had to struggle against the poets and their likes.
As Quran says:

"They [Satans] strain their hearing but most of them are liars

And the poets, those who have gone astray follow them

Have you not seen that they [poets] indeed wander aimlessly in every valley?

And that they say what they do not do?" Surah Shu'ara [The Poets] (26:223-225).

PRESS AND MEDIA

The media and press, audio and visual, have taken over the role of the magicians and poets of old in trying to divert the attention of people from seeking knowledge of the truth through use of their sight and hearing. It is no longer the magic of handful of magicians gathered from all over the ancient Egypt to challenge Moses rather a worldwide apparatus of magic that has penetrated in almost every house of the world which prevents the people from developing their ability to see and observe. Nor is anymore poets spread all across the Arabian Desert trying to lure people through their songs and lyrics away from listening to Quran - the word of God. Rather it is an organized mass media from one corner of the world to another which is hammering the ears of human beings so that they never listen to the voice of truth which is in scriptures or which is recited from the Throne of Almighty God. The children who are born in this kind of surrounding are deprived of any kind of opportunity of ever finding the truth themselves. They believe what the media tells them or shows them.

MUHAMMAD'S HEART (PEACE BE UPON HIM) SEES THE TRUTH

As we have seen in the story of Moses above, Prophet Muhammad peace be upon him also searched the truth. When God sent down the Holy Spirit to communicate His message to His servant Muhammad peace be upon him; the message first came in the form of a vision through the heart. It is not sleeping but waking vision. God informs us that his heart did not deny what it had seen.

"And then he inspired unto His slave what he inspired" Surah An Najam [The Star] (53:10-11).

Further on, God informs us that the sign which he saw as vision of the heart at the angle where two oceans meet called 'Qab a qawsein' on a straight line passing the two mountains, the same sign was presented to him once again near the lot tree of the further most limit. It coincided with God's commandment overspreading the lot tree. This time around he saw with his eyes that which he saw with his heart first. Quran says:

"While he [Gabriel] was in the horizon the most high

Then he drew near and lowered down

Till he was at the angle of two bows or even nearer

And then he inspired unto His slave what he inspired

Then his [Prophet Muhammad's] heart did not belie that which he saw

Are you then disputing with him about that which he saw

For indeed he [Prophet Muhammad] saw him [Gabriel] at the second descent

Besides the Lote-Tree of the farthest boundary

Besides it is garden of the welcoming

At a time when the Lote-Tree was being covered by that which was covering it

His sight did not wander nor did it transgress

Verily he saw the most great from among the signs of his Lord" Surah An Najam [The Star] (53:7-18).

FROM CONCEPTION TO REALIZATION:

Once again we see here this procedure from the conception of a vision to its realization. In the case of Moses peace be upon him we have seen, once we have conceived the vision of the fire in his heart he had made a resolute intention to go after his quest and that intention was followed with action and that action was crowned by success.

In the story of the Prophet Muhammad peace be upon him the details are little bit different. He initially developed a yearning to find God and out of that yearning grew a firm intention to seek that guidance and God's light which led him to take retreats in the cave of Hera. It was during those retreats that a spirit from God's commandment descended upon him: this incident is described in the first part of chapter Najam.

Between this vision and the next and the next one there was a lapse of many years which were years of struggle and hardship which culminated in the incident of Taif; whence the Prophet Muhammad peace be upon him and his companion Zaid were driven away by the people with stones. Shortly after this incident the prophet Muhammad peace be upon him was called by God for his nightly journey to heavens. This journey took him from Mecca to Jerusalem and from Jerusalem to the seventh Heaven; from seventh heaven to the Lot tree where at the second meeting with God's greatest sign took place.

In between the first vision by the heart and second vision through the eyes, lots of struggle and striving took place, until came the final fulfilment of the vision.

THE VISION OF IBRAHIM

In a similar manner when God wanted to introduce Ibrahim in to the rank of the people of certitude; He reversed the order of his (Ibrahim's PBUH) perceptions. The star, the moon, the sun which he used to see with his eyes first, now he began to see them through the vision of his heart "ru'yat".

"and thus We show Abraham the inner kingdom of the heavens and of the earth and so that he may become of those who have attained to certitude

So when the night engulfed him, he saw a star. He exclaimed "This is my Lord" But when it set, he said "I love not the things that set

Then when he saw the moon appearing in glory, he exclaimed "This is my Lord" But when it set, he said "If my Lord does not guide me, surely I will be of the people who have gone astray

But then when he saw the sun rising in glory, he exclaimed "This is my Lord; this is the most great" but when it set, he said "O my people! I indeed disavow all that you ascribe as partners to Him

I indeed, have set my face to the One who originated the heavens and the earth, in sincere devotion and I am not of those who ascribe partners to Him" Surah Al An'am [The Cattle] (6:75-79)

The ordinary things which he used to see with his eyes all time now has taken on a new meaning. Again the word ra'a (see by heart) is used rather the word "Absara". There when he saw the star, the moon, the sun it was all visions until he was confronted by God's manifestation (Tajally). Thereupon he exclaimed: "__ I have turned my face towards the one who at first created the heavens and the earth__". Thus he found his direction.

THE FREEZING SENSATION

Other details are given to us about Abraham when he first had his vision. When the stars caught his sight first he felt a freezing sensation to the point that he announced to the people around him that he was "sick". Quran says:

"When he came to his Lord with a peaceful heart

When he said to his father and his people "What is it that you are worshipping?

What? Are you seeking besides Allah a false god?

So what do you think about the Lord of the worlds?

Then he took a look into the stars" Surah As Saffat [Those Ranged in Ranks] (37:84-88).

That is not physical sickness that causes pain and discomfort, it is the nostalgia for a person or place that sees distant from us. It is a kind of homesickness that enthralls us created through the charming cool light of the stars.

THE AWAKENING OF THE HEART

It is said that human beings are sleeping and they wake up when they die. It means that their hearts are sleeping and their hearts are awakened only when they die and then see with both their hearts and their eyes.
It is also reported that Prophet Muhammad (peace be upon him) said:

"My eyes sleep but my heart sleeps not, likewise the prophets their eyes sleep but their hearts sleep not"

This prophetic saying makes it clear that sleep overtakes both hearts and eyes. For those whose hearts have truly awakened, sleep can only overtake their eyes to rest their bodies whereas their hearts remain active and vigilant; in which case whatever they experience during the period when their eyes sleep and their bodies rest is held as true and as valid as what they experience during the wakefulness of their eyes in addition to their hearts which remain awake at all times.
Meanwhile, the person whose heart is not awakened and only his eyes sleep and wake up, his awareness goes as far as his eyes see which is but a tiny fraction in comparison to the rest of the existence which lies beyond the scope of our eyes. What we don't see with our eyes is 99. 9% compared to what our eyes see, while all the remaining is accessible through the sight of our hearts. Our hearts, if awakened see both inner and outer existence while our eyes are limited to the outer and that is a very limited scope.

THE LIVING HEART

A heart which is called a living heart is one which has been awakened from its deep slumber and suddenly gains awareness about reality. It is sensitive, intuitive and knowing and is capable of distinguishing between truth and falsehood. A dead heart on the contrary is one which is dormant and completely unresponsive. It does not show regret for a wrong that has done or joy for the good/right it has done.
There is a story that King Abdul Malik of the Omayyad dynasty came to a scholar known in Medina and said to him " O so and so I have come to a stage whereby if I do something wrong I do not feel bad about it, and if I do something right I do not feel good about it. " The scholar said to him, "Your heart has completely died. "

DEGREES OF AWAKENING

The heart's awakening can be in varying degrees. Some hearts have three-quarter awakening some have half awakening and some one-quarter awakening while some have full awakening which is known as the great awakening (Al Fath Al Akbar). This great awakening coincides with the great remembrance whereby the awakened remembers God by heart perpetually. God says in Quran:

"Rehearse what has been inspired to you from the book and establish the prayer. Verily the prayer does restrain from the offensive and disgraceful acts and verily remembrance of Allah is the most great and Allah knows all that you fabricate" Surah Al Ankaboot [The Spider] (29:45)

HOW TO AWAKEN A HEART

God is the one who awakens a heart directly or indirectly through the agency of His vicegerents called warners or awakeners (نَذِير). The awakening is done in two ways, through iron or through fire. Through iron we mean the loud concussion between particles of iron which produce a sound like the ringing of alarms, hence the approach of some danger and therefore wakes up to find safety. By means of fire we mean the actual touch of fire which causes any sleeping person to jump out of sleep or a close contact situation either by seeing fire or feeling its intense heat. All these are means of making a sleeping person become wakeful and vigilant.

DIVINE MANIFESTATION

In other words when God wishes to awaken a person's heart He makes Himself manifested to him (Tajalli). The manifestation could be through a name of majesty or name of beauty. It all depends on God's intent. If He intends to awaken a person and make him a Warner accordingly, the manifestation will be majestic. A manifestation usually takes a medium as a siren, or could come in the form of a mountain like in the case of Moses (peace be upon him):

"So when Moses fulfilled the term and he set out at night with his family he perceived from the direction of Toor a fire. He said to his family "You wait. I have perceived a fire perhaps I will bring you from there a news [to guide you] or a brand from the fire so that you may warm yourselves" Surah Al Qasas [The Narrations] (28:29).

"and when Moses [finally] came unto Our tryst and his Lord spoke to him, he said "O my Lord! Make me see You looking at You". He said "You will never see Me (looking at Me) but look at the mountain. If it settles down in its place, then you will see Me" So when his Lord openly manifested Himself to the mountain, He made it level and Moses fell down unconscious and when he came back to consciousness he said "Glory be unto You. I have turned back to You in repentance and I am the first of those who are the believers" Surah Al A'raaf [The Heights] (7:143).

Or a tree as in the case of Prophet Muhammad (peace be upon him):

"At a time when the Lote-Tree was being covered by that which was covering it" Surah An Najm [The Star] (53:16),

Or luminaries as in the case of Abraham and Joseph:

"When Joseph said to his father "O my father I indeed saw in my dream eleven stars and the sun and the moon. I saw them in prostration to me" Surah Yusuf [Joseph] (12:4)

MOSES SEES FIRE

When God wanted to awaken Moses peace be upon him and send him as a Warner (نَذِير) to his people He made Himself manifested to him through the medium of a mountain (Toor). What Moses saw was a fire which was but an indication of a Majestic manifestation by God. The fire which Moses saw had already touched his heart which illuminates his heart into a broad day awakening. Next Moses went forward looking to find the fire with his eyes which he already found with his heart when he reached the mountain; there he met God who spoke to him. God had already awakened him before he came to meet Him so that His message does not fall on ears that are deaf and on a heart which is asleep. Moses, the awakened, came fully prepared to witness with his heart and hear with his ears what God was going to communicate to him:

"Has the story of Moses come to you

When he saw a fire he said to his family "tarry here. I have indeed perceived a fire maybe I can bring you from it a brand or I can find guidance at the fire

But when he come to it [the fire] he was called upon "O Moses"

Verily I am your Lord therefore take off your shoes for indeed you are in the sanctimonious valley of Tuwa

And I have chosen you so listen then to what is being inspired [to you]

Verily, I am Allah. There is no deity except I. Therefore serve me and establish prayer for my remembrance

Verily the hour is coming. I well-nigh hide it so that every soul is rewarded for that which it has endeavored

So do not let one who does not believe in it [the hour] and who has followed his desire hinder you from [remembering] it lest you perish" Surah Taha [Ta Ha] (20: 9-16).

Again at another place in Quran:

"When Moses said to his family "I have indeed perceived a fire and I will soon bring you from it a news [about the way] or I will bring you a burning brand so that you perhaps may warm yourselves"

And when he came over to it, he was called that "blessed be the one in the fire and those around it and glory be to Allah the Lord of the worlds

O Moses! Verily that is I, Allah, The All Mighty The All Wise

And that throw your stick" but when he saw it quaking as though it were a demon he turned his back and did not retrace his steps. "O Moses! Do not fear for verily messengers fear not in My presence Except one who has done wrong to his soul but then thereafter replaced wrong with good. Verily then I am Oft-Forgiving Most Merciful

And put your hand in your pocket and it will come out shining white not due to any harm. Among nine signs for the Pharaoh and his people. Verily they are a people who have transgressed against Allah's commandment"" Surah An Naml [The Ant] (27: 7-12)

"So when Moses fulfilled the term and he set out at night with his family he perceived from the direction of Toor a fire. He said to his family "You wait. I have perceived a fire perhaps I will bring you from there a news [to guide you] or a brand from the fire so that you may warm yourselves"

So when he came up to it he was called from the right bank of the valley in the blessed spot from the tree that "O Moses! Verily it is I, Allah, Lord of the worlds"

And that "Throw down your stick" So when he saw it quaking as through it was a jinn he turned his back in flight and did not retrace his steps. "O Moses come towards Me and fear not verily you are of those who are given safety"

Enter your hand through your pocket, it will come out shining white not due to any harm and draw your wing towards you from the fear. Those two are proofs from your Lord unto Pharaoh and his chieftains. Verily they were a people who transgressed against Allah's commandment" Surah Al Qasas [The Narrations] (28: 29-32).

THE OIL AND THE LAMP

In chapter An Nur of Quran God sets a parable for His light as it is in the heart of a believer. He calls the heart of a believer a lamp and the faith he has in his heart as the oil from an olive tree. This oil is so pure that it almost shines even without fire touching it. This pure oil is the example of who has attained purity of faith in God as Lord of Compassion and Mercy. However, the luminosity of this faith does not extend beyond itself because it has not been touch by the fire yet. It is a faith that has been awakened or ignited into full action so that it illuminates everything all around it, spreading life and light in all directions. It is to know that it only gains this dynamism when it is touched by the fire, and becomes two-fold light upon light. God says:

"Allah is the light of the heavens and of the earth. Likeness of His light is like a niche within which is a lamp and the lamp is within a glass and the glass looks like a brilliant star lit from a blessed olive tree that is neither in the east nor in the west. Its oil almost nearly illuminates even though fire has not touched it. It is a light upon a light. Allah guides unto His light whom He pleases and Allah sets forth the parables for the mankind and Allah is all knowing about everything" Surah An Nur [The Light] (24:35)

MASS AWAKENING

Once God has awakened someone by torching his lamp, it is a duty upon him to go about propagating the light and awakening others. This activity is known a Dawah, meaning "calling" to call other to come to life and light. It may range from simply walking among man so that if we perchance encounter anyone whose lamp is well oiled we merely torch it for him. This is the silent Dawah which is the commonest way of awakening the masses. However the awakener must stay in close contact with the masses mingle with them in the markets, on the streets, in various public places. The awakener may also captivate the attention of the masses through his good character and behavior. He may also awaken through his words which well reflect the reality in his heart while his actions must attest to his words. God says:

"O you who believe! Revere Allah and believe in His messenger. He will give you two measures from His mercy and He will make for you a light by which to walk and He will forgive you [your sins] and Allah is Oft-Forgiving Most Merciful" Surah Al Hadid [The Iron] (57:28)

"Is one who was dead then We brought him to life and We made a light for him by which he walks among the mankind like one whose likeness is in the darknesses and it is surely not going to get out of it. Thus We make seemly for the disbelievers all that they used to do" Surah Al An'aam [The Cattle] (6:122)

DEAD AND AWAKENING

An awakening is a resurrection and only those who are dead can be resurrected. Thus when God wishes to awaken someone he first puts him to death and then resurrects him. The magnitude of the awakening depends on the depth of the dying, if it was half dead then the awakening is half if it was a quarter dead then the awakening is quarterly and if the death was complete the result is a complete awakening which is known as the great awakening. Dead is synonymous here with unconditional surrender to the will of God. God says:

"Have you not seen your Lord how He causes the shadow to extend. Had He so wished, He would have caused it to be still then We cause the sun to lower on it"

"Then We will raise it up unto Us a gentle raising" Surah Al Furqan [The Criterion] (25:45-46)

"Is one who was dead then We brought him to life and We made a light for him by which he walks among the mankind like one whose likeness is in the darknesses and it is surely not going to get out of it. Thus We make seemly for the disbelievers all that they used to do" Surah Al An'aam [The Cattle] (6:122)

THE CHARACTERISTICS OF AWAKENERS

An awakener must combine within himself four characteristics which make him an accomplished awakener. The four are:

1. Be able to convey his message clearly by means of parables and allegorical representations. This kind of teaching brings tenderness into the hearts of the listeners and increases their faith.

2. Be a witness (شَهِيد) which means he must possess knowledge (عِلْم) which is based on certitude (عِلْمَ الْيَقِينِ). In this way there is no doubt in the message he communicates to other. Rather he removes all doubts from the hearts of his audience. As a true witness, he is capable of transposing the unseen into the seen.

3. Be a bringer of glad tidings (mubashir, basheer) bringing glad tidings regarding the imminent arrival of God's Mercy. In this way his role is similar to that of the cool breeze that precedes the down pour of the rain. As God says in Quran:

"And among His signs is that He sends the wind as bringers of glad tidings so that He may make you taste of his mercy so that the vessel may sail through his command and so that you may seek from His favor and perhaps that you may offer gratitude" Surah Ar Rum [The Romans] (30:46)

"Lo! He who guides you in the darknesses of the land and of the sea and He who sends the winds as bearers of good tidings ahead of His mercy. Is there a deity with Allah? Far exalted is Allah above all that they ascribe as partners to Him!" Surah An Naml [The Ant] (27:63).

As bringer of glad tidings he continues to strengthen the faith of the believers. Hence God represented by admonishing the prophet (peace be upon him) to give glad tidings to the believers because it does benefit them by strengthening their belief in the coming of God's Mercy.

4. Be a warner (Munzir, nazeer) who warns people and alerts them about the approach of the final hour which comes with God's judgement. As a result their hearts become wide awake vigilant and poised. This rude awakening in the heart is accompanied be some severe convulsions which cause the heart to throw of heaps of crusts and rust that has piled up in it due to inertia and indifference. This operation is known as the purification of the heart/soul (Tazkiah An nafs):

"And by a soul and how He extended its creation

And then He inspired it to know its transgression and its self-guard

Indeed he is prospered one who has sanctified it

And indeed he lost one who has stunted it" Surah Ash Shams [The Sun] (91:7-10).

"O prophet! We have sent you as a witness and as a bringer glad tidings and as a Warner

And as a caller to Allah by His leave and an illuminating lamp" Surah Al Ahzab [The Confederates] (33: 45-46)

TRAVELLING IN THE EARTH

Once an awakener has been given the awakening, it is not befitting to him to live a solitary life or remain a recluse or a hermit fixed in one stop. Rather an awakened individual must travel about in the earth, on land and sea, in the highlands and lowlands acquiring knowledge and also teaching it. Such tours in the earth are means for the awakened to get exposed to a multitude of God's signs which are spread in all directions in the earth. His knowledge increases as he gets more exposure. As God says in Quran:

"Soon We will show them Our sings on the horizons and within themselves until it becomes clear to them that verily He is the truth. Does it not suffice that your Lord, verily He is a witness over all things" Surah Fussilat [The Expounded] (41:53).

God also says:

"Say "Travel in the earth and look at how He started the creation. Then Allah will raise the last creation". Verily Allah has power over everything" Surah Al Ankaboot [The Spider] (29:20).

Verily these travels are meant to increase the awakened in knowledge by offering him the opportunity of encountering more reminders which activates his heart, his sight, his hearing and provokes him to reflect and ponder and thus increases the capacity of his faculties.
God says in Quran:

"Verily in that is truly a remembrance for anyone who has a heart and he keenly hearkens while he is a witness"Surah Qaf [Qaf] (50: 37).

The one who has a heart is one who can understand (عَقَل) or vision (رُؤْيَا) until his heart hears and obeys or who is witness through seeing with his sight. Through constant use and practice our faculties like heart, ear and sight increase in capacity and effectiveness. Each time a reminder comes (dhikr) we are faced with a new challenge in order for us to improve and excel in this regard. God says:

"Have they not peregrinated in the land so that they may come to acquire a heart by which to understand or ears by which to hear Lo! it is not the eyes in the head that go blind rather what goes blind are the hearts that are in the bosoms" Surah Al Hajj [The Pilgrimage] (22:46).

There God is admonishing the one who is awakened to travel in the earth so that as he gets exposed to God's signs which are reminders, his heart may grow in understanding (عَقَل) or his ears may grow in hearing, or that his eyes may grow in witnessing. Finally He makes comparison between the blindness of the heart and the blindness of the eyes. The eyes only see the outer, the world which is meant to pass. However, the heart sees everything which is true and will endure. One whose heart is blind but his eyes are seeing, he is truly blind. One whose heart is seeing but his eyes are blind, he is truly seeing.

CATEGORIES OF THE HEART

Muhammad, the messenger of Allah peace be upon him has divided the heart into four categories

1. A heart which is polished wherein is a bright lamp.
2. A heart which is tightly sealed up.
3. A heart which is inverted.
4. A heart which is equally divided in two halves.

The first is the heart of a believer who is awakened. The second is the heart of a disbeliever which was never opened onto faith. The third is the heart of a hypocrite. The fourth is a heart which is one part healthy and one part sick. The part which is healthy is watered with faith and the part which is sickly is watered with hypocrisy whichever dominates at the end determines the outcome.

AWAKENERS AND WARNERS

God has made it mandatory on the community of believers to pick out of its general membership a number of people who should devote themselves to learning and in-depth study of the scripture until they become awakened. This awakening is known as Fiqh (فقه) commonly translated as jurisprudence. It indeed means a heightened level of awareness that permits the awakened one (faqeeh) to know exactly the sense of a divine ordinance without transgression nor shortcoming. This exactitude in the interpretation of divine message is what is meant by fiqh. God says in Quran:

"and it is not right for the believers to go forth all together but if only a party goes forth out of every group of them in order to seek discernment in the religion and so that they may warn their people when they return back to them so that perhaps they will be on their guard" Surah At Tawbah [The Repentance] (9:122)

God thus admonishes the believers to select a number of them who will dedicate themselves to pursuing the in-depth study of scripture until they achieve true discernment in matters of the scripture and be able to interpret the meaning of the divine message with mathematical exactitude adding nothing nor taking anything away.

This precision in the interpretation of God's words is not within the reach of every lay believer in the community of the faithful. It is therefore incumbent upon the community as a whole to select a few among them and provide them with all the necessary means so that they could devote themselves wholeheartedly to the pursuit of knowledge. To this end they should be exempted from military services, payment of taxes and other related social obligations lest they become hindrances to their way to become awakeners and warners.

KNOWLEDGE AND WITNESSING

Another word which best describes the role of faqeeh (The awakened) in the community of faithful is the word 'witness'. He stands as witness among the members of the community pressing upon them the virtues of doing what is right and abstaining from wrongful deeds; the ultimate objective being to bring unto them awareness about the true boundaries set by God and highlighting the woes both individual and collective that result from transgressing God's boundaries and disobeying God's commandment.

As we can see this role of witnessing in the society is not within the range of every lay believer because the witness must be someone who has in depth understanding of the scripture and knows the precise interpretation of God's words this is what is known as fiqh and it takes someone whose heart is fully awakened and therefore he does not only hear the word but also witnesses what he hears; hearing is believing and witnessing is certainty. Therefore it is God himself who chooses from the larger community of the faithful those He wants to appoint over them as witness. God says:

"If pain touches you, then indeed pain touched the people like unto it. And those days We rotate between people and so that Allah may mark out those who believe and that He may take out the witnesses from among you and Allah loves not those who wrong their own souls" Surah Al' Imran [The Family of Imran] (3:140)

This verse describes two steps:

First, God separates those who have attained to faith from those who have not.

Secondly, from among those who have attained to faith, He chooses few as witnesses over them.

They are custodians of the knowledge of the book revealed by God and they stand as witnesses for the word of God:

"Verily they used to persist in their arrogance when they were told that there is no deity except Allah" Surah As Saffat [Those Ranged in Ranks] (37:35)

God says:

"Allah has witnessed that indeed there is no deity save He and the angels and people of the knowledge [have also witnessed] standing in uprightness. There is no deity save He, The All Mighty, The All Wise" Surah Al' Imran [The Family of Imran] (3:18).

We see from the foregoing that knowing and witnessing are closely connected and therefore there can be no witnessing without knowing as stated in Quran:

"Go back to your father and say 'O our father your son has indeed committed theft and we bear witness to nothing except that which we know nor are we the guardians to the unknown' Surah Yusuf [Joseph] (12:81).

You cannot therefore witness to what you know not which amounts to false witnessing (shahada az zoor).
God in this respect commands Prophet Muhammad peace be upon him saying:
"Therefore know that there is no god except Allah and seek forgiveness for your sins and for the believing men and women. For Allah knows all your places of movement and all your places of rest" Surah Muhammad [Muhammad] (47:19).
The commandment 'Know' is equal to witness and God therefore is commanding the Prophet to seek knowledge and become a true witness:

"O prophet! We have sent you as a witness and as a bringer glad tidings and as a warner

And as a caller to Allah by His leave and an illuminating lamp" Surah Al Ahzab [The Confederates] (33:45-46).

After knowing you become a witness and when you witness you become a warner and as warner you become awakener for it is through warning that people get awakened (حَذَر).

This verse furthermore sheds light on the role of the faqeeh after awakening, namely to become a witness and then a warner who spreads awakening and awareness in the society. It therefore defeats the purpose if a person after pursuing knowledge resigns himself to solitude and inaction rather he should go out in the society to witness and warn and spread awakening.

FIQH INSTITUTIONS

All human societies from ancient times to the present have all felt the need to select some of its members in order that they can dedicate themselves to pursuit of in depth study in the knowledge of the book. The recognition of this need has led different human societies to create institutions where advanced learning and in depth study of the knowledge of the book can be made available to those who have the desire to find true knowledge.
However these institutions have developed overtime in various ways even though the initial motive behind them is one. In this verse we see the development of monasteries or similar institutions in Hinduism, Buddhism, Judaism, Christianity and Islam. All those institutions were initially built in order to accommodate people who are seeking to pursue knowledge of the scripture and later on become witness in the society. The Quran speaks about Christian monasticism which developed after Jesus as a place of learning and meditation with a view to attain God's good pleasure (رِضْوَان).
God says:

"Then We made other messengers to follow on their footsteps and then We followed them with Jesus son of Mary and We gave him the gospel and We placed in the hearts of those who follow him tenderness and mercy but the monasticism which they invented, We did not prescribe it upon them save that they are doing it to seek the pleasure of Allah but they did not take care of it with a proper care so We gave to those who believe among them their rewards but many of them are renegades" Surah Al Hadid [The Iron] (57:27)

However these institutions of learning have progressively departed from their initial purpose. From being places where men find life and light and go forth spreading light and calling people to life and from being places where true knowledge is pursued to places of quiet prayer, solitary virtue and mere contemplation, they turned in to places where people who cannot cope with life outside, find refuge.
God says in Quran:

"By men whom neither trade nor traffic distracts from the remembrance of Allah or establishing prayer or paying sanctifying dues. They fear a day when the hearts and the sights will be upturned" Surah An Noor [The Light] (24:37)

These verses give us a precise description about the function of God's Houses and the type of people who frequent them. They are places where people come to remember God, establish prayer in congregation, and pay out their dues to the poorer member of community and the men who frequent them are merchants traders and men of different professions who rub shoulders with other men in the markets, bazars and other public places seeking the favours which God has written for them. It is these houses which God protects by the hands of men from those who wickedly seek to destroy them.
God says:

"It is they who are driven out of their home with no right just because they say "Allah is our Lord" Had it not been that Allah do push back one set of men by another, verily temples and churches and synagogues and mosques would have been pulled down wherein Allah's name is mentioned in abundance. Verily Allah will help those who help Him and Verily Allah is all powerful all mighty" Surah Al Hajj [The Pilgrimage] (22:40).

God takes it upon himself to protect these houses as long as they remain to be places where God's remembrance is celebrated and God's book is studied in view of enlightening other human beings. This failure on the part of these sacred places to fulfil their role in their respective societies has contributed to their widespread marginalisation.
It is reported that Prophet Muhammad peace be upon him said:
"The believer who mingled with people and exercise patience with them is better than the believer who does not"
Lack of tolerance, patience and forbearance has forced many of these institutions in to aloofness.
There are exceptions however vast majority of monasteries (Buddhists, Jewish, Christians) or khanqahs and zawiyas (Sufi retreats) have remained indifferent to sociopolitical conditions in the surroundings communities. Religion thereof should not be divorced from life otherwise it becomes anti life so instead of working with life it works against life instead of calling people to life it calls them to death:

"O you who believe! Respond to Allah and His Messenger, when He calls you to that which will give life to you; and know that Allah interposes in between a man and his heart, and that it is He to Whom you shall (all) be gathered " Surah Al Anfal [The Spoils of War] (8:24)

The forces that work against life can be categorized into three. These forces are known as darknesses. Our struggle therefore whether individual or collective consists in overcoming these forces which lurk in these darknesses in order to attain to true life that never diminish nor comes to an end. The third among the three darknesses is known as the greater darkness and the struggle against it is known as greater struggle (jihad al akbar).

1. The first darkness is called the darkness of sea. In this darkness reside the forces that call people to death. In other words they represent the hosts of death.
2. The second darkness is known as the darkness of the land. This darkness harbours the forces that wage war on people and kill them through the might of arms.
3. The third darkness is called the darkness of the city(between land and sea). This darkness harbours the forces that promote fitnah (confusion and sedition). It is also known as the darkness of the boundary(Al Barzakh).

The manner and the means of each struggle correspond to the nature of the darkness and the forces that inhabit that darkness.

As for the first darkness, it encompasses people to forces that lure people to death. As the word 'lure' indicates the hosts in this darkness do not resort to force in order to threaten and coerce their victim to accept their conditions. Rather they trap him in the prison of darkness by charming him with melodious words which freeze his entire being and deactivate his heart and hearing, sight and intuition (skin). As one in a trance he loses all awareness about himself and his surroundings. Each time he tries to rouse himself to pursue further life, their tragic tunes come to spell bound him and gradually change his desire for life to desire for death. The manifestation for this desire is known as grief (sorrow, sadness). Grief is indeed death before death for it causes the person who grieves neither truly live nor die. Hence the constant refrain in the Quran:

"If you do not help him then Allah did help him when those who disbelieved drove him out two of the two as the two were in the cave and when he said to his companion "grieve not verily Allah is with us". Thereupon Allah sent down His Sakeena upon him and strengthened him with hosts that you did not see and He made the word of those who disbelieve the lower and the word of Allah that is the higher and Allah is all mighty all wise" Surah Tawbah [The Repentance] (9:40).

"Do not be faint at heart and do not grieve for you are the ones with the upper hand if you are indeed believers" Surah Al'Imran [The Family of Imran] (3:139).

"And We inspired the mother of Moses that suckle him but if you have fear about him, then cast him in the river and do not fear and do not grieve for surely We are going to return him back to you and We are going to make him one of the messengers" Surah Al Qasas [The Narrations] (28:7).

"Lo! Verily The Allies of Allah, no fear comes upon them nor do they grieve" Surah Yunus [Jonah] (10:62).

"Do not be grieved by what they say. For all might indeed belongs to Allah. It is He who is The All Hearing, The All Knowing" Surah Yunus [Jonah] (10:65).

"So that you do not grieve over that which you fail to attain nor exult over that which you have achieved and Allah does not love any who is self-conceited self-vaunting" Surah Al Hadid [The Iron] (57:23).

Grief hinders a person from form and action in the pursuit of growth and expansion in living and thus restricts his movement and holds him like a prison, the geolrers of this prison are those among the humans and jinns who use words and images who drew people's attention towards things which are anti-life and anti-growth. Poets and magicians fall in to this category, unless such poets as call people to life and faith.
The only light which is able to dispel this darkness and route its lusts is the light of faith (nur ul Iman). It is the light which allows the believer to hear the call of the caller to life and responds immediately to the call. That response is an act of opening (fath فتح) which draws him out of darkness towards the light:

"Is one who was dead then We brought him to life and We made a light for him by which he walks among the mankind like one whose likeness is in the darknesses and it is surely not going to get out of it. Thus We make seemly for the disbelievers all that they used to do" Surah Al An'am (6:122)

"and give glad tidings to those who have believed and did righteous deeds that for them there will be gardens beneath which the rivers flow. Each time they are provided with a fruit therefrom, they would say "This is what we were provided with before" but it was brought to them similar to one another and for them there will be mates who are purified and they will abide therein forever" Surah Al Baqara [The Cow] (2:25)

The light of faith is as cool and as graceful as the light of stars. As the stars guide the travelers in the darkness of night until he reaches the brilliance of the day beginning with dawn, similarly the light of faith(nur ul Iman) guides the believer gently in the darkness of the sea or in the night and leads on slowly until he reaches the brilliance of certainty:

"Lo! He who guides you in the darknesses of the land and of the sea and He who sends the winds as bearers of good tidings ahead of His mercy. Is there a deity with Allah? Far exalted is Allah above all that they ascribe as partners to Him" Surah An Naml [The Ant] (27:63),

"and He it is who appointed for you the stars that you may be guided thereby in darknesses of the land and of the sea. Indeed We have detailed the signs for a people who know" Surah Al An'am [The Cattle] (6:97)

"[But,] verily, as for those who believe and do righteous deeds - their Lord guides them aright by means of their faith. Running rivers flow beneath them in gardens of bliss;" Surah Yunus [Jonah] (10:9).

In the second darkness, known as the darkness of the land or the wilderness (desert, country etc.) the hosts which reside here unlike the former ones, do not treat their victim with insidious gentleness in order to numb his senses and put him to sleep so that they can make him forget about his quest and keep him in the dark, rather the forces that aim to subdue their victim through fear of slaying.
They are the threatening and terrorizing. They cause their victim to go on wandering in the wilderness never finding peace or rest. Since they resort to might and aims to force their victim to wander away from the straight path which is the path of peace, they must be met with a greater might which is known as splendour of certitude (Nur ul yaqeen).

Fear (khawf خوف)which causes the heart to wander stems from doubt

and the surest means to repel fear is true certitude (يقين). The person

who has certitude does not have fear of anything created. Superstition, anxiety, panic attacks etc. are caused by fear which is caused by doubt.

Hence we fear what we do not know, however certitude (يقين) is a light

which makes everything unknown become known and therefore ward off the fear.
It is part of knowing, to know for certain, that God knows; when we know that God knows what we do not know is as though we know and we drive certitude from that knowing which ultimately gives us peace which is called salaam, Islam(peace, self-surrender).

In other words when we are certain that God knows, that certitude encourages us to surrender our affair entirely to God and that surrendering gives us the realisation of peace in our hearts. On the other hand when we doubt that God knows, that doubt encourages us to withhold our affair unto ourselves and that withholding gives us a realization of fear in our hearts making us errant and restless.
As the light of faith (Iman) resembles the light of stars in terms of grace and coolness but also in terms of multiplicity because there can be as many manners of belief as there can be stars. But the light of Islam is however single and radiant like the sun which overpowers everything with its majesty and splendour:

"They seek to put out the light of Allah with their mouths but Allah with all intent wants to complete His light even though the disbelievers are averse

He it is who sent His messenger with the guidance and with religion of the truth so that He may make it triumph over all the religion even though those who ascribe partners to Allah are averse" Surah Tawbah [Repentance] (9:32-33).

"And who does greater wrong to his own soul than one who contrives the lie against Allah while he is being called to self-surrender and Allah does not guide the people who have done wrong to their own souls

"They want to extinguish the light of Allah with their mouths but Allah is going to fulfill His light even though the disbelievers may be averse to it"

"He it is who sent His messenger with the guidance and religion of the truth so that He may make it prevail over the religion all of it even though those who ascribe partners to Allah may be averse to it" Surah Saff [The Battle Array] (61:7-9)

From the struggle for faith (Iman) to the struggle for peace (Islam) the person comes to the greatest struggle against the most complex darkness which is the darkness of the boundary. The boundary symbolizes the crucible wherein elements are mixed together to form a compound product. Similarly the city is like a crucible wherein people of diverse characteristics, some wild and aggressive as the denizens of the wild desert or sly and treacherous as the inhabitants of the sea, all melt together in the crucible of the city. Out of this miscegenation comes a hybrid kind of humans in a very advanced stage of alienation from their true nature. In the face of this darkness a single light doesn't stand a chance of winning. The light of iman which overcame the darkness of the sea cannot succeed alone nor can the light of certitude which triumphed over the darkness of the wilderness.

It will take a compound light to undo a compound darkness. This compound light is invested by God in a human who has realized double expansion both vertical and horizontal. He is thus enlightened twice: vertically by means of his spirit and horizontally by means of his soul.

The light that originates from the commandment (أمر) comes into his heart through the spirit and the one that originates from the creation(خلق) comes into the heart through his soul. These lights are called the light of commandment (amr أمر) and the light of remembrance (zikr ذكر) respectively. He is both commanded and reminded. At this point a person is known to have attained excellence.

He obeys God's commandment and submitted to his will (Tasleem) and this submission earns him in return peace in his heart. On the other hand he listens to what God reminds him and believes in it and that belief in return earns him tranquility (sukoon سكون) in his heart. The heart where peace and tranquility are combined is truly a heart in excellence:

"We said "O fire be cool and peace upon Abraham" Surah Al Anbiya [The Prophets] (21:69).

Eventually from the fusion of the two lights: the light of certitude which proceeds from the commandment by the intermediary of the spirit and the light of faith which proceeds from the remembrance by the intermediary of our souls, as a compound light is formed within our hearts known as baseera (Insight بصيرة).

Those who carry this compound light within their hearts are known as people of the heart, in other words people of the middle or the boundary because the heart stands as a boundary between commandment and remembrance:

"Have they not peregrinated in the land so that they may come to acquire a heart by which to understand or ears by which to hear Lo! it is not the eyes in the head that go blind rather what goes blind are the hearts that are in the bosoms" Surah Al Hajj [The Pilgrimage] (22:46).

"Say "This is my way. I call on to Allah [I am] on a clear vision me and whoever follows me and glory be unto Allah for I am not of those who ascribe partners to Him" Surah Yusuf [Joseph] (12:108)

The people of the heart (ulul albaab, ahlul qaloob, ulul absaar) Surah Qaf (50:37), Surah Ibrahim [Abraham] (14:52), Surah Al Imran(3:13) who are endowed with the compound light of baseera are the ones who are charged by God to undertake the reform of human beings as they emerge with the complex fabric of this life in the cities, they are given two mandates: to command and to remind. In this capacity they exercise the function of people of commandment (ulul amr) who are empowered by God to command others on the one hand while on the other hand they exercise the function of the people of remembrance (ahl dhikr) who also are empowered by God to remind others:

"O you who believe! Obey Allah and obey the messenger and the people of the commandment among you. But if you disagree about anything, then refer it back to Allah and to the messenger if you indeed believe in Allah and in the last day. That is better and most excellent in interpretation"Surah An Nisa [The Women] (4:59)

"Allah has witnessed that indeed there is no deity save He and the angels and people of the knowledge [have also witnessed] standing in uprightness. There is no deity save He, The All Mighty, The All Wise"Surah Al Imran [The Family of Imran] (3:18)

"And We did not send anyone before you except men unto whom We sent our inspiration so ask the people of remembrance if you do not know" Surah An Nahl [The Bee] (16: 43)

"We never sent before you except men whom We inspired [you who disbelieve] ask then the people of remembrance if you do not know" Surah Al Anbiya [The Prophets] (21:7).

By combining the capabilities of both the people of commandment as well as the people of remembrance they are in a better position to administer the complex nature of the neo human breed in the cities through reminding and commanding.
They command them to submit to the will of God through the commandment (Tasleem)which if they do they will find peace in their hearts while on the other hand they also remind them to think well of God and believe in His good promise which if they do they will find tranquility in their hearts:

"Those who follow the messenger, the unlettered prophet, whom they find written with them in the Torah and in the Gospel. He commands them to the kind things and he forbids them from the wicked things and he makes clean things lawful for them and he makes the unclean things unlawful for them and he takes away their heavy burdens from them as well as the fetters which were upon them. As for those who believe in him, and honour him and help him and follow the light which was sent down with him, they it is who are the ones who will prosper" Surah Al A'raf [The Heights] (7:157), Surah Al Imran [The Family Of Imran] (3:110), Surah Al Imran (3:104), Surah Hajj [The pilgrimage] (22:46), Surah Luqman [Luqman] (31:17).

In the end when they succeed to bring peace (salam) and tranquility (sakeena) into the hearts of people their mission to reform people is considered fulfilled and in conclusion God says to them;

"Declared unlawful upon you is the dead-meat and the blood and the flesh of the swine and all the sacrifices which were invoked in other than the name of Allah and the strangled animals and the one beaten to death and the one fallen from high and the one gored to death and the ones eaten by beasts of prey except ones that you have slaughtered before their death and all those which are sacrificed on the altars of immolation and that you divide by means of the raffles; all that is a renegation. Today those who disbelieve have lost all hopes about your religion therefore do not defer to them but defer to Me. Today I have perfected your religion for you and I have completed My blessings on you and I have chosen submission to Allah as a religion for you. But whoever is driven by necessity through extreme hunger not through inclination to impiety then verily Allah is Oft-Forgiving All Merciful" Surah Al Maida [The Table Spread] (5:3)

UNIVERSALS AND PARTICULARS

By universal we mean a rule that is true and applicable at all times and at all places. Therefore there are two true universals – the universal time and the universal place. These are also known as absolutes: the absolute time and the absolute place.
However any rule that does not apply at all times and at all places, but rather it applies in one time not another or in one place but not another, that rule is not universal and it is not absolutely true. It may be true but it is relatively true, that is to say that it only holds true if it relates to a particular context in time or space. Whenever it is taken out of that context it does not hold good, that is not an absolute and has no universal attribute, Such rules are called particulars. Their validity and applicability is limited to one particular context and not beyond.

The Two Universals:

There are only two universals: the universal time and the universal space. The universal space is the one space that God created at the beginning. This is the space expansion. It is one continuum of space that has no ending. This one space forms the back-frame against which all particular spaces were created, including the arsh (throne), the heavens (and what they contain), the earth (and what it contains), and everything in between the heavens and the earth, from the smallest to the largest.
The universal time is the one time that God created from the beginning and it extends to infinity. This is the time expansion. This one time forms the background against which all particular times were created, including days, months, years, hours, night and day, morning and evening, etc.

The Mother of the Book (أُمّ الكتاب)

Now the parable of these two universals that serve like backgrounds unto the particulars is like an extensive white board and a correspondingly extensive writing tool called the pen. They are the universal board and the universal pen. Upon the universal board such are universal truths that are valid and applicable at all times and at all places, and they last eternally.

The universal board is called the Mother of the Book. Just as a mother's womb carries what God has created therein, likewise the Mother of the Book carries the written word of God. The universal pen is the Father of the Book. The Book, therefore, is what God has written in the universal board by the universal pen. The universal board is the Mother of the book and the universal pen is the Father of the book. What is written by the universal pen upon the universal board is also universal and eternal and they are not subject to change or alteration:

"It is they who believed and used to guard their souls out of reverence for Allah" Surah Yunus [Jonah] (10:63)

"Those who are left behind would say "When you set out to take hold of booties, let us follow you" They want to change the word of Allah. Say "You will never follow us" Thus has Allah said before but they will say "You are only begrudging us" Nay they discern not except a little" Surah Fath [The Victory] (48:15)

However, anything that is not written by the universal pen (Father of the Book) upon the universal board (Mother of the Book) is not eternal and can be changed:

"Allah effaces what He pleases and confirms [what He pleases] and with Him is the mother of the book" Surah Ar Ra'd [The Thunder] (13:39)

Therefore whatever is written in the universal book entrenched in the Mother of the Book cannot admit addition nor subtraction. It is complete and eternal and therefore sealed.
Whenever the Qur'an refers to the book as 'that book', the reference is to the "universal book" as in the opening of chapters Baqara, Al Imran, Naml, A'raf, Yunus, Yusuf, Hud, Ra'd, Ibrahim, Hijr etc. in Quran.

NUN AND THE PEN

The universal board and pen are also known under other names in the Qur'an; for example, 'nun ن, which is the mother of the book and al Qalam_ اَلْقَلَمِ, which is the pen, the father of the book. The book is referred to as "what they write____ وَمَايَسْطُرُونَ" The writing is in a present progressive tense to signify that writing is infinite and it is eternal, incorporating the past and the present and the future:

"Nun. By the pen and all that they write" Surah Al Qalam [The Pen] (68:1)

LAW AL MAHFOOZ

"Lawh al Mahfooz", the preserved tablet, is another name given to the mother of the book or the universal board. It is called so because whatever is written therein is universal, eternal and lies beyond the reach of factors of change:

"Nay! It is a Quran most glorious!" Surah Al Buruj [The Stations of stars] (85:21).

"Verily it is We Ourselves who have sent down the remembrance and verily it is We who will protect it" Surah Al Hijr [The Rocky Tract] (15:9)

THE REMEMBRANCE (ذِكْر)

The Remembrance (al-dhikr) with the definite article also refers to the book written by the universal pen on the universal tablet. Individual books or writings were then transcribed from that universal. In reference to the Psalms of David, God says that we have transcribed in the Psalms after the Remembrance, meaning that a portion of the Remembrance was transcribed in the Psalms.
God says in Quran:

"And We indeed wrote in the psalms after the remembrance that the earth will be inherited by my righteous servants " Surah Al Anbiya [The Prophets] (21:105)

THE TWO PLANES

The two planes or dimensions are the time plane and the space plane. The time plane is horizontal and runs east to west. The space plane is vertical and it runs earth to heaven or down and up as opposed to right to left. When the east and west are rolled into one so that one is neither easterly nor westerly, neither right nor left -- rather east and west in one single dimension -- the result of this fusion is the one dimensional universal time and it is universal so it is eternal. This is the eternity of time. Such is the parable of the light of God, which is neither easterly nor westerly (Ayah noor):

"Allah is the light of the heavens and of the earth. Likeness of His light is like a niche within which is a lamp and the lamp is within a glass and the glass looks like a brilliant star lit from a blessed olive tree that is neither in the east nor in the west. Its oil almost nearly illuminates even though fire has not touched it. It is a light upon a light. Allah guides unto His light whom He pleases and Allah sets forth the parables for the mankind and Allah is all knowing about everything" Surah An Nur [The Light] (24:35).

In a like manner the earth and the heaven rolled into one, so that the total is neither earthly nor heavenly as they were once before partition:

"Do those who disbelieve not perceive that the heavens and the earth were both joined together then we parted them asunder and from the water We made every living thing. Will they not then believe" Surah Al Anbiya [The Prophets] (21:30)

The total therefore is one single dimension. This single dimension is the one dimensional universal space and as it is universal so it is eternal. This is the eternity of space. This is why God is referred to as the light of the heavens and earth, that is the heaven and earth as one not as two, in Surah An Nur(24:35).
If the slave witnesses the oneness of time and the oneness of space he/she has indeed witnessed the prime beginning when time was one and space was one and everything was one. That is you cannot count more than one. The one that is universal and true and eternally true. This witnessing of the beginning leads to the witnessing of the One God as His light spreads on the One extended creation to eternity. This witnessing is only at the reach of those who are steadfast (have sabr صَبْر) in their quest of seeking the Face of their Lord.
It is said that those who are steadfast are given their reward without count, because through their patience and steadfastness, they succeeded in reaching beyond the world of counting to the one of beyond count. The beginning when everything was rolled into one (before the spreading into many-ness). This is the first period. The period of no count (bighair hisab_ بِغَيْرِ حِسَاب):

"Say "O my slaves who believe, revere your Lord" For those who act in excellence in this world, there is an excellent reward for them and Allah's earth is wide. Only those who are steadfast and patient are given their reward in full without calculation"Surah Az Zumar [The Crowds] (39:10)

Here is the manifestation of the Truth and he witnesses the Truth by the Truth and hears the Truth by the Truth. The means and the end are one. Since there is only oneness, the means and the end cannot be distinct. The Truth is the means and the Truth is the end.

THE LIGHT UPON LIGHT

God is the light of the heavens and the earth, and He is the light of the easts and the wests:

"Lord of the heavens and of the earth and all that is in between them and Lord of the rising points of the sun" Surah Saffat [Those Ranged in Ranks] (37:5).

"(Lord of the two easts and the Lord of the two wests"Surah Ar Rahman [The Most Gracious] (55:17)

His light in the heavens and the earth is His commandment, which is in between the heavens and the earth and by it they are held together. The commandment is called "Amr":

"He pronounces the commandment from the heaven down to the earth then it rises up to Him in a day which is worth thousand years from that you count" Surah As Sajda [The Prostration] (32:5).

"Allah it is He who created seven heavens and from the earth likes of them. The commandment keeps comes down between them so that you may know that Allah has power over everything and that Allah has encompassed everything in knowledge" Surah At Talaq [The Divorce] (65:12)

It runs through the earth and heavens as the blood runs through the vessels of the human body. Its movement through the earths and the heaven is identical to the blood circulation in our body. This is the universal light of the vertical dimension or space light.

The second light is the light of God in the easts and the wests or the light of His creation. It is called "Khalq". So if the Amr is like blood in the body, the Khalq is the body through which that blood circulates and runs. If the khalq is in between the east and west so the Amr is in between earth and heaven and they cut across each, this one going up and down while this one is going east to west or this one going from down up and this one going from west to east and they're cutting across each other like two stones striking against each other or two electric wires striking against each other, there the two lights fuse together and give rise to a light that is neither easterly nor westerly, neither earthly nor heavenly. This is the light upon light. With this light all times become present and all places become presence.

THE TWO PERCEPTIONS

Out of the cross breeding of these two lights comes two intertwined perceptions or visions. One is called certainty or yaqeen (يَقِين) and the other is called intelligence or 'aql (عقل). With the perception of certainty (yaqeen يَقِين) we can perceive singleness and with perception of intelligence (Aql) we can perceive distinction and differentiation. The "Baseera" (insight) or the vision of the heart results from the amalgamation of both. God has commanded us to keep a fine balance between the two perceptions without letting anyone transgress the measure (Tughyaan طُغْيَان) or fall short of the measure (Takhseer تَخْسِير):

"And the heaven He raised it up and He brought down the balance

So that you do not transgress in the balance

And establish the weight with equity and do not fall short of the balance" Surah Ar Rahman [The Most Gracious] (55:7-9)

With these two perceptions in fine balance, our vision is not uni-dimensional it is universal. We not only see vertically or horizontally but vertically and horizontally simultaneously. Those who lack this comprehensive vision, they are not able to have true visions of God since their vision is dualistic. That is, it is one-sided and God's light is not one-sided, it is all-dimensional. This is the witnessing of unity, there is no way to get to the vision of the One Creator if we haven't realized the unity of the creation. By this unity we mean evenness of time and space and the absolute balance of the yaqeen (certaintyيَقِين), which is the sum of all parts of faith and aql (intelligence), which is the sum of all parts of knowledge.

DEATH AND LIFE

God created the creation in two stages. The first stage or the first period is the creation of death. This is referred to as the first creation (Khalq-al Awwal, An-nash'at-al-ula):

"Were we ever worned out by the first creation? Nay! They now are in confusion about a new creation" Surah Qaf [Qaf] (50:15)

"You indeed do know the first creation why then do you not remember?" Surah Al Waqi'a [The Inevitable Event] (56:62)

"Or any other form of creation that looks great in your heart and they will say "who is going to bring us back" say "the one who created you the first time" they will nod their heads to you and say "when will that be" say "perhaps it will be soon"Surah Al Isra [The Night Journey] (17:51)

Death is created, and since it is created it cannot be considered as non-being or nothingness. Death is simply another plane of creation. Death is characterized by plainness, absolute stillness and absolute silence. For this reason, death is also known as yaqeen(يَقِين__certainty). Once we reach certainty (or death) our quest is reached, so there is no further reason to continue to move; for movement is a symptom of seeking. When there is no seeking there is no moving. Absence of movement is stillness.
Secondly when we reach the end of the quest and everything becomes plain and obvious then speech becomes redundant and seeing replaces speaking. Absence of speaking leads to absolute silence. Stillness is a sign of certainty as well as silence; and certainty and death are synonymous:

"And worship [supplicate] your Lord until certitude comes to you" Surah Al Hijr [The Rocky Tract] (15:99)

Out of the stillness and silence results a third characteristic of certainty or death and that is the "Fixity of gaze". That is, the gaze does not wander. As long as the gaze wanders the quest has not been reached. When the quest is reached the gaze does not wander anymore, it becomes fixed and immovable. It has found its fulfillment (Ridwan). Silence leads to listening and hearing and non-wandering of the gaze leads to fixing the look and to seeing. These characteristics of yaqeen are manifested outwardly in our hearing, our sight and our skin, and inwardly in our heart.
The heart, like our bodies, must be silent, still and fixed in gaze. Only then can a person be said to be among those who have achieved certitude (yaqeen). At this point the hearing and seeing are in reverse order. It is seeing and hearing:

"If only you could see when the evildoers are going to bend their heads low in the presence of their Lord saying "O our Lord! We have seen and we have heard so send us back [to the earth] and we shall work righteousness for verily we now have certitude" Surah As Sajda [The Prostration] (32:12)

As long as the hearing precedes seeing, then certainty has not been reached:

"and thus We show Abraham the inner kingdom of the heavens and of the earth and so that he may become of those who have attained to certitude" Surah Al An'am [The Cattle] (6:75)

The qualities of seeing and hearing, silence and listening, and stillness are the characteristics of the first creation or the first fitrah, namely the creation or fitrah of death. If at any time the slave returns back to the first state of creation of fitrah then he has attained certitude (yaqeen).
At the first fitrah the slave witnesses his own beginning and how God began the creation:

"Say "Travel in the earth and look at how He started the creation. Then Allah will raise the last creation". Verily Allah has power over everything" Surah Al Ankabut [The Spider] (29:20)

With the witnessing of the beginning of creation and how it all began the witnessing slave has now entered into the greatest Remembrance (Dhikr-al-Akbar). This witnessing of the beginning of creation and how the beginning of creation started is not possible except by returning to the first creation of fitrah, which is the period of death or yaqeen (certainty). Hence the statement of Prophet Muhammad peace be upon him:
"know that you will not see your Lord till you die"
And he, peace be upon him also said:
"Ihsaan (excellence) is to worship God as though you see Him and if you were not seeing Him, He sees you. "
It is only in going back to the first fitrah that we can worship God as though we see Him.
God also challenges those who claim to love Him and want to be his friend by saying:

"Say "O you who have adhered to Judaism! If you claim that you are friends to Allah to the exclusion of other people then yearn for death if you are indeed true in your claim" Surah Al Jumu'a [The Friday] (62:6)

In other words, desire to return to your fitrah__ to the first state of your creation. If you return to this state you have reached certitude. Once you have reached certitude, then you have become the "wali " friend or beloved of God. Therefore "wilayah" to be a wali (a friend, a beloved) of God entails that one returns to his first fitrah. If he/she returns to his/her first fitrah he/she has become a wali ولى.
With the resumption of one's first fitrah, mercy (Rahma) automatically descends upon the wali. With the descent of mercy (Rahma), all forms of God's blessings like (amn أَمْن) security which is the absence of fear and (Qarar (قَرَار), Tuma'nia) stability, tranquility as opposed to wandering and agitation. For this reason God says:

"Lo! Verily The Allies of Allah, no fear comes upon them nor do they grieve" Surah Yunus [Jonah] (10:62)

As long as the slave is in his first fitrah, the mercy (رَحْمَة) continually descends upon him. The Rahma (mercy) gravitates towards the first fitrah and as long the fitrah is preserved the continuous influx of Rahma is guaranteed. If there is any shift or alteration in the fitrah, then Rahma(رَحْمَة) ceases to descend. If the Rahma ceases to come then of course the individual will be exposed to agents that will cause him pain, in the form of fear, distress, anxiety and feelings of insecurity and instability. These are the symptoms of darkness and contraction.
God says that whatever good happens to you it is from God and whatever harm happens to you it is from yourself:

"Whatever happens to you of good is surely from Allah and whatever happens to you from evil, then it is from your own soul and We have sent you as a messenger for the mankind and it suffices that Allah is all witnessing" Surah An Nisa [The Women] (4:79)

Meaning that if the soul retains its fitrah____the way God first created it, it will attract good towards it such as mercy (رَحْمَة) and kindness.

If the fitrah of the soul is alienated, then Rahma will past from it and harm will befall it. It all depends on the disposition of the soul. If the soul retains its fitrah it will certainly invite good upon itself. If the soul alters its fitrah, it will attract harm. Harm is simply the absence of good (Rahma) and darkness is the absence of light.
If the soul however reverts back to its fitrah, harm will leave and good will come. God, therefore, says:

"That is because Allah is never going to change a blessing which He has bestowed on a people until they change what is in their souls and verily Allah is all hearing all knowing" Surah Al Anfaal [The Spoils of War] (8:53)

That means all souls are created first time provided with the blessings of God. They will continue to enjoy these God-given blessings as long as they do not alter the condition, meaning the fitrah of their souls. If they change the first state of their souls, then the blessings will move away and the curses will come:

"Before him and behind him are angels who take turns. They protect him from the commandment of Allah and Allah does not change the state of a people until they change the state of their souls and when Allah wills to bring harm to a people there is none who can turn it away. They will have no one to be an ally for them besides Him" Surah Ar Ra'd [The Thunder] (13:11)

"And those who ascribed partners to Allah said "If Allah had willed we would not have worshipped aught besides Him neither us nor our fathers neither had we prohibited anything without his commandment. Thus did those before them act but is there anything on the messengers except the clear conveyance [of message]"Surah An Nahl [The Bee] (16:35)

Therefore God is not to blame for the harms that come to them, it is men who are to blame for changing the conditions. When we encounter hardships it is well we always look into our souls and see if we have caused any change so that we can fix the problem swiftly.

THE PARABLE OF THE CITY

God sets forth the parable of a city that enjoyed a stable, secure and happy life. They enjoyed this blissful state of being simply because of the unaltered state of their fitrah. God continued to shower down his blessings upon the city and they continued to live under the protection and the bountiful provisions of God, until the moment when they began to alienate their fitrah and change their ways.
They changed mercifulness, which is part of fitrah, to mercilessness. They changed humility to arrogance; they changed peace for war, gentleness for hardness, soft-heartedness for harsh-heartedness. In this way they have altered their fitrah and the conditions of their souls changing the attendant blessings also were exchanged for affliction:

"Allah sets an example of a township which was enjoying security and tranquility and its provision was coming to it abundantly from every place but it turned ungrateful to the blessings of Allah so Allah made it taste [cover it with] the dress of hunger and fear because of that which they used to perpetrate" Surah An Nahl [The Bee] (16:112)

THE CITY OF JONAH

The city of Yunus was such a city as had gone against the fitrah. God sent Yunus (peace be upon him) to call them back to their fitrah but they refused to listen to his words of good counsel. As their alienation from their fitrah increased so the consequences increased. Their adversities were multiplied.

At one point, Prophet Yunus could see that the cloud of mercy, that at one time cast its shade over the people of the city and rained down God's blessings, had gone away. Another cloud, thick, dark, that gave no shade and rained down no rain of mercy, replaced it. Prophet Yunus saw that God's mercy was replaced by His anger and that His wrath was about to strike the city for changing the way of God, which is the fitrah. Prophet Yunus feared for himself and fled in anger. He left his flock unattended when they needed him the most. Is not God's mercy greater than His anger? Then let God's anger, therefore, be repelled by His mercy. For those who believe in His mercy, this is the only option.

In the meantime, the people of the city, pleaded out of pain and distress to God's mercy and reverted to their fitrah. Most often pain and distress brings people back to their fitrah and they sincerely repent. When they reverted to their fitrah and repented sincerely the cloud of chastisement went away and the clouds of mercy came back. It sent down a rain that quenched their thirst, washed away their sins and removed their woes.

REVERSION TO FITRAH

Indeed there are no moments of interruption in the course of a human being's existence from the time he was brought to life to the time he dies. As he is created, his actions are also created with him. Therefore he never ceases to act till the moment of death. God says:

"Whilst it is Allah who created you and all that you work" Surah Saffat [Those Ranged in Ranks] (37:96)

Therefore the creative process continues from the beginning of life to death.

However, the quality of his actions will depend on the state of his fitrah. If the act was done while the person, who is the agent of the action, was in the normal disposition of his fitrah, then that act will be qualified as a good act. The act comes out identical to the fitrah of the actor in equal proportions, no more no less. A good act emanates from us as an exact copy of our soul in fitrah, it thus ascends to the heaven and gets through the door of heaven. This entry is possible solely because the door of heaven is adjusted to the size of a sound soul that is a soul in its fitrah, no more no less. If our act emanates out of us as a copy of our sound soul then it can fit through the door of heaven and the angels will grant it entrance:

"Whoever is seeking the might, verily all the might is for Allah. To Him mounts up the good word and the good deed He raises it up and those who are scheming the evil deeds, for them is a formidable punishment and the scheme of this, it is this that is going to waste" Surah Fatir [The Originator] (35:10)

On the other hand if he performs an act while the fitrah of his soul is in an altered state -- that is his soul is out of fitrah disposition -- then any act performed in this state will be qualified as a bad act. This means, that act will emanate from the individual in the form of the alienated fitrah. It will be excessive in proportion or in short of right proportion. The act goes up to the heaven in this manner and when it reaches the door it does not fit in perfectly through the door of heaven. Therefore it is rejected. When it is rejected it is sent back to where it originated from, namely the actor of the act.

This is what is meant when they say that your sin fall back on you and your evil deeds come back to haunt you. By the law of gravity the speed of a falling object is greater than the speed of the shooting object and also the impact is greater. A man's evil deeds keep on falling back on his head until it builds up to the sky like a cloud above his head:

"The corruption has appeared in the land and in the sea because of that which the hands of mankind have wrought so that He make them taste part of what they have worked perhaps they may return" Surah Ar Rum [The Romans] (30:41)

"So give unto the one who is near in kinship his right and to the needy and to the way farer. That is best for those who are seeking the face of Allah and it is they who are the prosperous" Surah Ar Rum [The Romans] (30:38)

But if they turn away, surely We have not sent you as a keeper over them. All that is on you is but a clear deliverance [of the message]. And when We indeed give the human being a taste of a mercy from Us, he exults in it. But when ill befalls them because of that which their hands have sent forth, then truly the human being is full of ingratitude!" Surah Ash Shura [The Consultation] (42:48)

If however, God wants him/her to repent and revert back to his fitrah, he will let the weight of his misdeeds oppress him and squeeze him to the point that in extreme distress he/she will cry out to God and repent. If he sincerely reverts to his fitrah and asks for pardon and forgiveness he will be forgiven no matter the amount of his sins and God may turn all that misdeeds into good deeds:

"Except such a one who turns back to Allah in repentance and reaffirms his belief and does a righteous deed. Verily it is they whose evil deeds are replaced by Allah with virtuous deeds and Allah surely is Oft-Forgiving Most Merciful" Surah Al Furqan [The Criterion] (25:70)

However if he/she persists in acting with his/her distorted fitrah and continues in his ways till the last day and did not take heed or warning from God and everyone do get at least a warning or two in a year:

"Do they not see that they are tried every year once or twice but then they repent not nor do they bring themselves to remembrance" Surah At Tawba [The Repentance] (9:126)

If death finds him/her in this state of altered disposition then when his soul departs from his body, it finds the thick impenetrable cloud of his misdeeds hanging above him and stretching to the heavens. Neither his deeds nor his soul, in its deformed state, can enter through the door of heaven. When the person is finally buried, his evil deeds come and hang above his grave like an ill-omen cloud. It provides him with neither shade nor gives him coolness, nor does the rain of mercy rain upon him. Rather it oppresses him with its weight, squeezes him and rains down hail and fire upon him in his grave. It is nothing but his deeds:

"Verily those who belied Our signs and acted arrogantly towards them, for them the doors of the heaven will not be opened and they will not enter the garden until the camel passes through the eye of the needle and thus do We requite the evildoers

There will be for them from hell a cradle and from above them a shower [of brimstone] and thus We requite those who wrong their own souls"Surah Al A'raaf [The Heights] (7:40-41)

Likewise as the righteous performs righteous deeds, which means acts that are performed while the heart in its right disposition which is its fitrah or first sound nature. His acts emanate from him and ascend into the heaven. That good deed is presented to God and in return mercy (Rahma) and kindness (Birr) are sent down upon the doer of the good deed. So as one deed goes up, a sort of counter value descends. God says:

"Is the reward for excellence other than the excellence?" Surah Ar Rahman [The Most Gracious] (55:60)

But certainly God's kindness is greater than the good deed of the slave. However "the reward of wrong is wrong like unto it", that is the wrong is the reward of itself, it is your own deed given back to you:

"And the price for ill is ill like unto it but one who pardons and amends, indeed his reward is upon Allah. Verily He does not love the wrongdoers" Surah Ash Shura [The Consultation] (42:40)

As this exchange is carried on between the Master and His slave a link builds up between them. The link is a cloud of mercy that builds over the head of the righteous (مُحْسِن) and extends into the heavens; it rains, it thunders, it lightens. From this cloud rains water, ice and hail all harmoniously descend upon the slave with lightning and thunder as described in surah Nur verse 43:

"Have you not seen that Allah draws a cloud then He puts it together then He reduces it into a pile and then you see the rain coming out from between it and He sends down from the heaven from mountains therein from hail with which He strikes whom He pleases and averts from whom He pleases. The brilliance of its lightning almost nearly snatches away the sights" Surah An Nur [The Light] (24:43)

If the righteous dies, his soul ascends into this cloud of light carried by air into the presence of the Almighty and then into the paradise. If he is buried, this cloud of mercy comes and stands above his grave and a pillar of light extends from his grave well into the heaven. In his grave while awaiting the final resurrection and the judgment day, he continues to receive the shower of God's mercy upon him.

PERVERSION OF FITRAH

Perversion or alteration of the fitrah is called sickness or disease in the heart. We notice that God does not say sickness of the heart but rather sickness in the heart. For the heart (قَلْب) is within the bosom (صَدْر)and within the heart is something known as zar or sirr or fuad الْفُؤَاد. It is the essence of our being called our fitrah which is also the source of the intentions we make.

If this inside is faulty, certainly whatever we do comes out faulty. If it is healthy, then whatever act we do comes out healthy and wholesome according to the fitrah. This is the root of our being and our actions are its fruits. If the tree is sickly the fruits will come out sickly. Similarly, if the tree is healthy the fruits will come out healthy. For this reason Prophet Muhammad peace be upon him (SAW) says:

"God does not look at your outward forms or colors but rather at your hearts and your deeds. "

Simply because our deeds are the fruits of our heart's condition. If the heart is in a healthy condition, our deeds emerge healthy and if our hearts are in a sickly condition our deeds emerge sickly.

In considering the healthiness or sickliness of hearts and deeds, two things are not taken into consideration: the outward form and the color. These two have no influence on the outcome of our actions. It is rather that the actions emanating from a well-disposed heart meaning a heart which has preserved the condition in which God created it at first. Therefore a healthy action emanating from a healthy heart is like a healthy fruit growing on a healthy tree. It will exhibit two qualities:

1. It will have a good taste
2. It will have a sweet fragrance.

Therefore the form and color have no bearing on the condition of our hearts and our actions. Form and color are completely irrelevant to God and that is why He does not look at them. For when God looks at something, it means that the object has received a sign of approval from God and God has granted its permissions to remain forever in God's favor and pleasure (رِضْوَان). It is a thing remembered by God. On the contrary whatever God turns away His look from, it is a sign that, the object has not received God's approval and God is not pleased with it. It has earned God's displeasure (غَضَب). It is a thing not remembered by God and so it is consigned to oblivion:

"Say "If I am misguided, then my misguidance is only against my own soul but if I am guided it is because of what my Lord has revealed unto me. Verily He is all hearing all near" Surah Qaf [Qaf] (34:50)

"Taste then [the punishment of hellfire] for your forgetting of the meeting of this day of yours. We too have forgotten you and taste the punishment of ever lastingness for all that you used to do" Surah As Sajda [The Prostration] (32:14)

"They will not fight you altogether except in fortified townships or from behind walls. Their strife is mighty among them. You think that they are united altogether but their hearts are divergent. That is because they are a people who do not understand" Surah Al Hashr [The Gathering] (59:15)

To remember God is to turn towards Him and to forget Him is to turn away from Him. Likewise God's remembrance of something means God is turning His face towards that thing and forgetting it means turning away from it. To remember something means to turn your face towards that thing, remembrance is therefore synonymous with pleasure and satisfaction. Those who are satisfied with God, God is satisfied with them, they turn to Him and He turns to them:

"Their reward is with their Lord gardens of eternal bliss under which rivers flow to abide therein forever. Allah is pleased with them and they are pleased with Him. That is for anyone who defers to his Lord" Surah Al Bayyina [The Clear Evidence] (98:8)

FORM AND COLOR

Form and color are the result of two phases in the creation of the human being; namely the blood and the flesh. Form and color are therefore the product of blood and flesh and since blood and flesh are irrelevant to God, their produces -- color and form -- are also irrelevant to God. And God says in chapter Hajj of Quran:

"Their flesh never reaches Allah nor their bloods but the God reverence from you reaches up to Him. Thus He has made them subservient to you so that you may extol the grandeur of Allah for the reason that He has guided you and give glad tidings to the ones who act in excellence" Surah Al Hajj [The Pilgrimage] (22:37)

Meaning that blood, flesh, and what emanates from them, does not reach unto God. Rather what comes from within the heart reaches up to Him. The Prophet also says:

"God does not look at your color and your form, but at your heart and your actions"

That is, the actions that emanate from the heart are looked at by God, however actions that emanates from the flesh and blood and characterized by form and color cannot mount up to God. No sooner it leaves the doer and ascends then it comes back crashing on his head. For every deed, good or bad, returns to its origins.

CONDITIONS OF ACCEPTANCE

Therefore acts that are good in their own right may not qualify for acceptance by God because of the manner of the execution. If a charity is given out of flesh and blood it certainly cannot get to God, for God does not accept anything that carries the mark of the flesh and blood. If the same act of charity emanated from the fitrah of the giver and was executed out of heart, it will reach up to God. Such an act that emanates out of a good heart is sweet and fragrant, while the one that emanates out of a sick heart dominated by flesh and blood comes out smelling like blood and flesh and therefore the door of heaven is not open to such deeds.

THE FIRST PART AND THE LAST PART OF HUMAN CREATION

God says that He created death and life to see whom among you will excel in deeds:

"He who created the death and the life so that He may try you and mark out who among you is most excellent in work and He it is The All Mighty the Oft-Forgiving" Surah Al Mulk [The Dominion] (67:2)

Death has preceded life, so death belongs to the first phase of creation (fitrah) and life belongs to the second or last. When God first created the "nafs" called the "soul" from the clay he drenched it into the water of death or (مَوْت), also known as certitude (يَقِين__yaqeen). This water comes from the ocean of the unseen (غَيْب). This water is distinct from the water named "life" out of which living things emerged. This water belongs to the second phase of formation that is the phase of blood and flesh.

MULTIPLE WAYS BUT SINGLE GUIDANCE

(A Comparative Study of the Way of Moses and the Way of Muhammad, Peace be upon them)
There are two ways but one guidance. The single guidance is the guidance of peace (salam) and the two ways are the waterway and the sandway. Each of these two ways represents the two essences out of which God created the human being, namely water and dust.
God says in Quran:

"And it is He who created the human being from the water and has made for him kinship through blood and through marriage and verily your Lord encompasses everything in his power " Surah Al-Furqan [The criterion] (25:54).

At another place in Quran God says:

"And among His signs is that He created you from dust and then Lo! you are wholesome human beings spreading out all around [in the earth]" Surah Ar-Rum [The Romans] (30:20).

The dust is a grain of sand and the water is a drop of liquid. Each of these two substances has a distinctive nature; water is wet and moist while dust is dry. The human being therefore is a compound in nature by virtue of the wet and dry substances he/she is made of.
This composite nature of the human being is both an advantage and a challenge for him. The challenge lies in the fact that each of the two components competes for supremacy within the human kingdom. The dry component tends to make him more masculine and the wet component tends to make him more feminine.
The advantage however lies in his success to strike a balance between the two and thereby realizing the purpose of his life: to find the perfect balance.
God says in Quran:

"And the heaven He raised it up and He brought down the balance

"So that you do not transgress in the balance"

And establish the weight with equity and do not fall short of the balance " Surah Ar-Rahman [The Most Gracious] (55:7-9)

HUMAN FACULTIES

In view of the two essential components of human nature, the human faculties can also be categorized under two sections: the ones that are dry in nature and the others that are wet in nature.

The two most important of all human faculties are sight and hearing. The sight falls under the dry section and the hearing under the wet section. These two senses—hearing and sight—constitute the two most common means through which the human being is guided in his life and for his quest for self-realization. Either he follows what he sees or he follows what he hears.

In seeing, he is an active follower and participant, but in hearing he is passive. This means that the energy and vibrations are projected in different directions when we look and when we listen.

In looking, the energy is projected outwardly meaning that the energy explodes and spreads. It is a dispersion mode. However, in listening, the energy is projected in the opposite direction, that is inwardly. In this case, the energy implodes and congregates. Therefore the mode of conveyance of energy depends on the nature of the conveyor. If the conductor of the energy is wet and moist, the energy is attracted and preserved, but if the conductor is dry, the energy is dispersed and spread.

The ears therefore are wet conveyors and they act like a magnet. They attract energy and preserve it, but the eyes which are dry conveyors push out the energy and spread it. In this way the energy flows in through our ears and it is then called hearing and thereafter when it rises up to the eyes, the eyes spread and disperse it.

To fulfill their respective functions, God therefore structured the ears in a single form and structured the eyes in a dual form. In this manner because the ears are odd in structure, they are able to attract vibrations in a holistic, synthetic way without analyzing it. The analyzing part is the duty of the eyes because of their dual nature. They break things down into their minute details and analyze them and then spread them.

DAY AND NIGHT

Like our hearing and our sight, Allah has made the day and the night into two conductors of His Light. The night is a wet conductor or passive conductor, and the day is a dry and active conductor. The night gathers the light energy and the day spreads it. The day therefore is bright because the light is spreading out and the night is dark because the light energy is collected and kept in.
God says in Quran:

"And it is He who made the night for you a dress and the sleep for you a rest and has made the day a resurrection" Surah Al Furqan [The Criterion] (25:47)

In this way, the night resembles the magnet and the day resembles the silver. The magnet has the capacity to contract and attract and the silver has the capacity to expand and disperse. Thus, the night particles are called 'khunnas' خنس and the day particles are called 'kunnas' كنس.

"So I do swear by the Khunnas [heavy and slow moving night particles]

And by the flowing Kunnas [light and fast moving day particles]

And by the night when its darkness comes along

And by the dawn when it breathes out " Surah At-Takwir [The Roll Up] (81:15-18)

The night inhales the magnetic electrons and the day exhales them as silver electrons. In this way when we breathe in we draw magnetic electrons and when we breathe out we spread silver electrons.

SUNLIGHT AND ENERGY FIELDS

The Sun alternates between its day attire and night attire. Its night attire being the dark green magnetic particles that stick to the sun's face in countless numbers as the sun bathes itself in the western magnetic field called A'inin Hami'a(عَيْنٍ حَمِئَةٍ) (or 'in the dark spring').

Thus, as the sun plunges itself to prostrate into the magnetic ocean of the khunnas (خنس)__in the west___it comes seeded all over with fine tiny magnetic particles and these dark green magnetic particles concentrate and pull together the solar energy and thus attract it inward. Night therefore becomes a period of stillness and silence.

Conversely, the day attire of the sun is constituted of the body of silvery particles that are released at sunrise as the sun courses through the silver field of the east. These particles are called the 'kunnas'(كنس) or 'waraqa' which means silver. They are both dry in nature and fast in motion. As they move and race, their inter-friction raises a huge blanket of dust and because of their lightness and transparency, they spread the solar energy and disperse it, causing the radiance of the day. However, at the same time, as they cover the sun's face and spread its energy, they overlay the dark-green magnetic particles. Thus, the magnetic particles constitute the inner dress of the sun and the silver particles constitute the outer dress.

SAKINAH (TRANQUILITY سَكِينَة) AND BASEERAH(INSIGHT_بَصِيرَة)

Sakinah (سَكِينَة) and Baseerah (بَصِيرَة) respectively refer to the inner and outer attires of the sun. Each of these attires produces a different impact on the heart of the human being. The sakinah attire brings stillness and silence into our hearts and thus sleep and ultimately brings death. On the other hand, the Baseera attire brings wakefulness to our hearts and therefore motion and action, all characteristics of a wakeful being. Therefore, as the sun progresses in its daytime course it increases in brightness and wakefulness, but as its daily course draws to its conclusion towards the evening, it gets stripped of its day attire. (*"A Sign for them is the night, We stripped it of the day, and behold they are in darkness"*). As the sun's day dress is taken away, the sun begins its nocturnal course.

However, while the sun is guided during its daytime course by the means of its baseerah (بَصِيرَة), which means its clarity of sight, it is guided in the night by the sakinah (سَكِينَة). In the night, the sun can no more depend on its eyes for guidance. Eyes have no use in the darkness. Thus, the sun stops relying on its eyes for guidance in the darkness and opts for its ears. In the darkness, sound vibrations are released from the magnetic field that guides the attentive listener in the right direction.

This is what happens to us when we sleep or when we die, we can hear but we can't see. As for those who are well-trained in the art of listening, their souls are guided in the right direction during their sleep or at their death.
As for those who have not learned to listen well, their souls cannot discern or detect the subtle vibrations of the call of the Caller unto God, the Light and Life. Since they cannot detect the good call, but in vain they try to find the way out with their eyes. Thus they remain locked up in the wilderness of the darkness, bewildered and confused.

STATIONS OF JOURNEY

Therefore, the journey on the way of God comprises periods of darkness (night) and periods of brightness (day). Each period calls for a specific modality of journeying. The appropriate tools must be applied to the appropriate period.
When the journey is during the day, the traveler must rely on his sight for guidance. There is no point trying to use your hearing to see God when you are in a broad daylight. However, when the darkness of the night falls in, the traveler must switch over to his hearing for guidance.
Therefore, one must be flexible in switching back and forth to the right mode of guidance according to the prevailing circumstances. This adaptability to the circumstances is what constitutes the guidance of peace.
You will find no peace in the darkness unless you resort to your hearing for guidance and the same in the brightness unless you fall back on your sense of seeing, because peace lies in being in tune with God's order of things. So to seek guidance through your hearing while it is day, is going counter to God's order and the same when one tries to go by his sight in the darkness—he will also be going in reverse of God's order. Neither will find peace.
God says in Quran:

" Go hence both of you to him and say both of you "We are messengers of your Lord therefore send with us the children of Israel and do not afflict them with any more punishment. Verily we have come to you with a sign from Your Lord and the peace is on him who follows the guidance " Surah Taha [Taha] (20:47).

That means the one who follows the guidance of the day in the day and the guidance of the night in the night.

THE SEA AND THE DESERT

The journey through the night is like unto a journey across water. To succeed in travelling through water, the traveller—like a fish—must master two skills: the skill of swimming and the skill of good listening and good hearing.

God, Who created everything and guided them, guides the fish in the water through its hearing and the fish in the water never go by their sight. So, sight does not constitute a useful tool in travelling in the water. Listening is a flow movement and a good listener is a good swimmer. Darkness therefore is a mass of water and to cross it one must swim through it. That swimming is done through the sense of hearing. Your hearing will rightly guide you through if you know how to listen well. Definitely it is useless to try to use your sense of seeing in those circumstances, for sight is for a walker and not for a swimmer.

On the other hand, when the journey is across the desert which is a dry space, it is therefore reasonable to use the dry sense which is sight. It is now time to walk and not to crawl and to go by the sight and not by the hearing. Actually if you try to go by your hearing in this circumstance, you are trying to swim your way across the desert (land) and most certainly you cannot go very far.

God says:

"and He it is who appointed for you the stars that you may be guided thereby in darknesses of the land and of the sea. Indeed We have detailed the signs for a people who know" Surah Al An'am [The Cattle] (6:97).

That means He guides you through the darkness of land through your sight and in the darkness of the sea through your hearing. This means that in a watery environment you should be still and silent and let the magnetic essence in you expand and attract the energy or light inward because projecting the energy out in these circumstances will be a mere waste. Therefore in the water you should merely draw in and listen, which will enable you to flow along with the vibrations in the sea and therefore right follow the course of water. The journey through water is a return journey while the journey across the land is a forward journey. So the sight takes you forward and the hearing takes you backward.

In this way you don't travel only one way—you both return to God and go forward to meet Him. The travelers in general are either returners or forwarders.

The returners are those who characteristically journey through their sense of hearing while the forwarders are the opposite. However, the best group are the ones who combine both modes of journeying. They move forward and they move backward and they travel both day and night and therefore they are twice guided and twice in peace.
As for the two separate groups, one group travels only by night and the day doesn't count for them while the other group travels only by day and the night doesn't count for them.
The third group are the ones who explore both the land and the sea and then employ the appropriate guidance in the appropriate setting. They go by the Sakinah in the darkness of the sea and by the Baseerah in the darkness of the land.

DHIKR (REMEMBRANCE) AND SHUKR(GRATITUDE)

Dhikr(ذِكْر) is remembrance and Shukr(شُكْر) is gratitude and God has made the day and the night for the purpose of remembrance (dhikr) and gratitude (shukr). Night is the time of dhikr and day is the time of shukr.
However, like the day follows the night and the night follows the day, dhikr and shukr must alternate. Dhikr(ذِكْر) means remembrance and remembrance always refers to the past, not to the future. Dhikr therefore involves a journey into the past—it is a backward journey through the water. Remembrance and the act of listening are therefore intertwined. If you listen you will remember, meaning you will remember the past and if you remember the past then you certainly will know whence you came and how to go back. Remembrance should therefore be followed by returning (Tawbah).
After the returning is done, then the next phase begins that of Shukr (gratitude شُكْر) which means to seek God's Face and His Pleasure. This second phase of the journey is a daytime journey and you must set your face straight ahead in seeking God's Face. This is an upward journey, the land journey as opposed to the downward journey, which is the sea journey. Hence, backward and downward are synonymous, forward and upward are synonymous as well.

The conduit for backward and downward is wet while the conduit for forward and upward movement is dry. It follows therefore that at the moment of remembrance (dhikr) we are in expansion and absorption, and therefore in such moments one must refrain from all forms of contraction and dispersion like walking or talking. One should be still and silent until the remembrance is completed.
God says in Quran:

"Far exalted is Allah The King, The Truth and do not be in haste with the Quran before its revelation to you is consummated and say "O My Lord increase me in knowledge" " Surah Taha [Taha] (20:114)

Also God says:

"Do not move your tongue with it in order to hasten with it" Surah Al Qiyamah [The Resurrection] (75:16)

After its completion one must immediately engage in gratitude (شُكْر) which means setting out on the quest of finding God's Face and Pleasure. The energy that is gathered in the time of remembrance must be dispensed and utilized in the time of Shukr. For this reason God often says in the Qur'an:

"Then He made him even and breathed His spirit into him and He made for you the hearing the sight and the understanding. Little is the thanks that you offer" Surah As Sajda [The Prostration] (32:9)

This means that the slave must first return back to God but to return back to God he must go the same way he came. He came from water into life ("*Out of water We made everything come to life*"), therefore he must return back through the water. He cannot return back in any other way. But to return back he needs to remember how he came. Therefore he must need to listen well.
If he listens well, God will remind him and once he has remembered he must immediately return in the manner that the whales travel back to the spot they were born, to die. In exactly the same way, a human being must know his way back to where he was first created at the Throne of God on the water. The whales are capable of remembering their birthplace and returning to it simply because they are endowed with good listening skills and God guides them through their hearing back to their beginning.

Once this backward journey is completed and the slave returns to God, God will breathe in him a new spirit as at the first time. This Spirit within the human being actualizes into three forms of light or energy depending on the conduit. In the ears it turns into hearing; in the eyes it turns into sight and in the heart it turns into understanding (fuad).
Thus equipped with these three forms of energy the human being begins another round of his quest for the Face of God and His Pleasure.

THE GUIDANCE OF FAITH

The guidance of faith means the guidance through hearing. Whoever is guided through hearing certainly has faith which means that he does remember God and does return back to him. However it is not possible to remember God unless one first knows how to listen.
Through listening remembrance comes and through remembrance the downward journey is undertaken. That downward journey is what is known as faith (Iman). Faith therefore is an inward journey of the soul downstream into the primal water in which the souls were first created. This plunging of the soul into the primal water constitutes the purification of the soul (Tahara). This is a reunion of our watery essence with its source. In that purification anything lies in its reintegration with its original source. Water goes back to water and it turns pure. Dust goes back to dust and it comes out clean and the Spirit goes back to God.

THE TRINITY

The roots of the trinity go back to the consideration of these three essences that constitute the human kingdom.
The first essence is dust, the second is water and the third is the Spirit. These three represent respectively the father, the mother, and the Holy Spirit.

Water is the symbol of motherhood, dust is the symbol of fatherhood and the Spirit comes from the Word of God. The dust and water are both vehicles for the Spirit whilst they live in unison. When they separate each returns back to its world. The Spirit is from the commandment and it returns to the world of commandment. Both the dust and the water belong to the world of creation but each belongs to a different segment of it. Water belongs to the lower part of the world of creation which is west—earth; and dust belongs to the upper part which is east—heaven. Therefore when there is separation each of the three returns to its source—water to water, dust to dust and Spirit to God. The seed goes back to the father; the liquid substance goes back to the mother and the Spirit goes back to the Lord of Commandment:

"Your Lord indeed is Allah, Who created the heavens and the earth in six periods, then He established His presence over the throne. He causes the night to cover the day following it in swift pursuit and (He created) the sun and the moon, and the stars subservient through His commandment. Lo! for Him is the creation and the commandment. Blessed is Allah Lord of the worlds" Surah Al A'raf [The Heights] (7:54).

THE PURPOSE OF THE UNION

There is a purpose when God put together these otherwise three disparate essences. The three have a common goal and a unique objective to achieve. That common goal is to work together in peace and harmony to produce a being that is neither dust nor water nor spirit, but transcends all three and becomes a non-denominational entity of fine understanding (Fuad) and equilibrium (Taqwa). This fourth is the sublimated essence out of the three basic essences of dust, water and Spirit. The one sublimated essence out of the three is the final product and the child (son) of the three.

However, in order to reach this state one needs to master the discipline of self-dissolution. That means the ability to dissolve his composite self by sending each part to its original source. The dust goes back to dust, the water goes back to water and the Spirit goes back to the commandment. The return of dust to dust is known as "Tawbah" or repentance. The return of water to water is known as "Iman" or faith. The return of the Spirit back to the commandment is through goodly actions (A'mal Salih). These three steps are referred to in several verses of the Qur'an:

"Except such a one who turns back to Allah in repentance and reaffirms his belief and does a righteous deed. Verily it is they whose evil deeds are replaced by Allah with virtuous deeds and Allah surely is Oft-Forgiving Most Merciful

And whoever turns back to Allah in repentance and does a righteous deed, he therefore does truly turn to Allah with a complete repentance" Surah Al Furqan [The Criterion] (25:70-71)

"But whoever turns to Allah in repentance and he affirms his believe and does a righteous deed, then perhaps he might be of those who prosper" Surah Al Qasas [The Narrations] (28:67)

"And I am truly most forgiving to whom who repents and believes and does a righteous deed and keeps on the right guidance" Surah Taha [Taha] (20:82)

WHAT IS THERE BEYOND THE TRUTH

Is there aught beyond the truth? The answer is: nothing. The truth is the end and the beginning and there is nothing before or after the truth. To continue to seek after having the truth is indeed going astray. Such a seeker is like someone who after finding the fresh pool of water continues to seek after a mirage. Certainly he is searching for nothing and his effort is in vain. God says:

"That indeed it is Allah your Lord, The Truth. What is there beyond the truth other than misguidance? Whither then are you turned" Surah Yunus [Jonah] (10:32)

BEFORE AND AFTER

Our life spans over two periods:

1) The period when we continue searching for the truth until we find it.

2) The period when we find the truth up till death.

During the first period we don't know what the truth really is but we do know of its existence. We therefore sincerely keep looking for it until we find it. Finding it depends on one's sincere desire to find it and God crowns our efforts with success due to our sincerity. Sincerity (or Sidq صِدْق) is therefore the principal requirement for one who is seeking. In a prophetic tradition it is narrated that Prophet Muhammad peace and blessings of God be upon him said:

"I urge you to be sincere because sincerity leads to piety and piety (birr) leads to paradise____A man continues to be sincere(in faith) and continues to search with all intent and purpose for sincerity(in faith) till he is ordained a sincere believer in God's presence. "

Sincerity in faith ultimately leads you to paradise (jannah) which is true. That paradise is narrated in a prophetic tradition:

"You (God) is the Truth, Your word is the Truth, Your promise is the Truth, meeting with You is True, paradise (jannah)is true, hellfire is true_____"

However it takes one to have sincere belief in the truth to find the truth. Our sincere belief in the truth can eventually lead us to realize the truth in any of its above mentioned forms. It may lead us to God Himself. It may lead us to His word, it may lead us to His promise, it may lead us to the meeting with God, it may lead us to paradise and it may lead us to find the hellfire; to whichever one among them your sincere faith leads you, you certainly have found the truth and therefore have found God.

But then after finding the truth what do we do? Here begins the second period of our journey in life. It is the period wherein we are no more searching for the truth but that we have found it and our duty now is to hold fast unto it with all our being. We walk by it, we hold by it, we see by it and we hear by it. It must fill our entire hearing so that we cannot hear anything else. It must fill our entire sight so that we cannot see anything else. It must fill our hands entirely so that we cannot hold unto anything else. It must cover our feet entirely so that we cannot walk by anything else. It must saturate our feeling so that we feel only by it. It must fill our heart entirely so that there is no room for anything else. It must fill our spirit our soul and our body entirely.

From this point on we are in the truth and it is with us. We keep abreast with it neither falling behind it nor going ahead of it; in total harmony and concordance with the truth. It is an everlasting companionship which keeps us in perpetual growth with excellence.

ROOT OF MISGUIDANCE

The root of misguidance lies in seeking after finding hence many people have gone astray for seeking after something when they already found the truth; for what then is there after light other than darkness or what then is there after certainty other than doubt or what then is there after being, other than non being.

One who continues to seek after finding the truth is guilty of ingratitude (kufr)and\or misguidance(dalaal ضَلَال). He is ungrateful because of negligence towards a blessing conferred upon him by God. Truth is the sum of all blessings; whoever found the truth found all blessings. Therefore seeking for something else after finding the truth is an act of negligence towards God's blessings which is considered ingratitude (kufr). God says:

"Have you not seen those who have changed the blessing of Allah into ingratitude and caused their people to dwell in the home of perdition" Surah Ibrahim [Abraham] (14:28).

God says:

"Ask the children of Israel how many a clear sign We gave unto them and whosoever alienates the blessings of Allah after that they had come unto him then verily Allah is most formidable in retribution" Surah Al Baqarah [The Cow] (2:211).

Ingratitude (kufr) towards God's blessings turns that blessing into a woe and torment.
God says:
"God does not change what is with people until people change what is with themselves" meaning that God does not change a blessing on people into tribulation unless they change their gratitude into ingratitude.
God says:

"And whatever good is happening to you is from Allah but whenever harm touches you surely it is to Him that you flee for help" Surah An Nahl [The Bee] (16:53)

Therefore ingratitude changes a blessing onto a torment.
God says:

"That is because Allah is never going to change a blessing which He has bestowed on a people until they change what is in their souls and verily Allah is all hearing all knowing"Surah Al Anfaal [The Spoils of War] (8:53).

Secondly such a person is gone astray, because after finding the truth which is light he passed it by wandering into darkness. It is befitting for him that when he found the light he should hold on to that light and with it explores the darkness:

"Lo! He who guides you in the darknesses of the land and of the sea and He who sends the winds as bearers of good tidings ahead of His mercy. Is there a deity with Allah? Far exalted is Allah above all that they ascribe as partners to Him" Surah An Naml [The Ant] (27:63).

In chapter Al An'am God says:

"Say "It is Allah who saves you from it and from all other afflictions" but then here you are ascribing partners to Him" Surah Al An'am [The Cattle] (6:64).

This journey that every soul must undertake; takes them across darkness of the land and darkness of the sea so that without true light he will remain ever bewildered in the darkness:

"Is one who was dead then We brought him to life and We made a light for him by which he walks among the mankind like one whose likeness is in the darknesses and it is surely not going to get out of it. Thus We make seemly for the disbelievers all that they used to do" Surah Al An'am [The Cattle] (6:122).

(ACKNOWLEDGEMENT) MA'ARIFAH AND (GRATITUDE) SHUKR

In order for someone to show gratitude for a favour of God he must first recognize it as blessing from God. Hence the fatalistic link between cognizance (Ma'rifah) and gratitude (shukr). In other words there can be no gratitude if there is no cognizance. Once a person recognizes a favour of God he has indeed found the truth and from then on it is duty upon him to hold fast on it and look after it well which constitutes gratitude.
However Ma'rifah "cognizance" begins with returning back to one's true nature called fitrah. In other words one knows himself truly when he/she reverts back to his/her true nature as the way God first made him. The state he was in until then is a changed state called 'tabdeel تبديل ' or 'taghyeerتغيير' or 'inkaar' إنكار'.
There is no possibility for anyone to recognize the truth until unless he be first in his true nature while in his/her true nature he recognizes everything that comes his way as it came from God, true and unaltered. However if human being himself happens to be in a changed (tabdeel) state he projects his own state on everything else.
Thus God says:

"That is because Allah is never going to change a blessing which He has bestowed on a people until they change what is in their souls and verily Allah is all hearing all knowing" Surah Al Anfaal [The Spoils of War] (8:53)

Meaning that if their sound disposition (fitrah) changes, then everything else changes in consequence, if their sound disposition remains intact then everything else remains well. Therefore change does not mean changing the human being into what he has not been rather changing him back what he was before.

FITRAH: self in which God created him at first, once this change is done truth is recognized immediately and everything good follows. For wellbeing and happiness are incidental on the fitrah. If one's true nature prevails he is well and happy but if his true nature alters the wellness and happiness depart from him.

God says:

"The blessing that is with you is from Allah but if harm touches it is to Him that you flee_"

Meaning that God blessing is with you on account of your being in your fitrah but then when harm touches you because of changing your fitrah which caused you to disregard God's favour you flee back to God whereby you return back to your fitrah and then the pain departs from you.

In the course of a person's life there are moments when he regains his true nature and for a moment he gets a feeling of extreme happiness and wellness. It lasts for a moment and then he changes again to his troubled state. The human being in his true nature is supposed to feel that way at all times. But due to the fact he cannot maintain his true nature(fitrah) he relapses in grief and fear and other symptoms of a troubled state.

God says:

"They recognize the blessing of Allah but then they deny it and most of them are ungrateful" Surah An Nahl [The Bee] (16:83)

They may happen to recognize God's favour which they are in their true disposition but then their disposition suddenly changes and they no more recognize God's favour nor show gratitude for Him. However these moments of self –integrity do not prevail at all times therefore they must be seized upon and turned into advantage while they last.

God says:

"The day when the veil from Saaq [Allah's radiance] will be removed and they will be called to the prostration but they will not be able to do it" Surah Al Qalam [The Pen] (68:42)

It means that they used to have moments of self-integrity when they felt well and happy and they were supposed to take advantage of those good moments of wellness and happiness to do an act of grace that will surely get accepted by God since any act that one does on his true nature gets accepted by God. On the other hand any act that one does while he is not in his true nature it is surely rejected by God.

God says:

"and relate unto them by the truth the news of the two sons of Adam when both of them offered an offering but it was accepted from one of them and it was not accepted from the other. He said "I will surely kill you" He said "Allah only accepts from those who revere Him"Surah Al Maida[The Table spread] (5:27).

On the contrary God does not accepts from those who have not safeguarded their true nature for God is wholesome and does not accept except what is wholesome.

QUALITY NOT QUANTITY

In the eyes of God there is no comparison between what is wholesome even though little and what is un wholesome (khabeeth خبيث) even though abundant.
God says:

"Say "Not equal are the bad and the good even though the abundance of the bad incite your admiration. So revere Allah, O people of the heart so that perhaps you may prosper." Surah Al Maidah [The Table Spread] (5:100)

The deed of one man in his true nature (fitrah) outweighs the deed of thousand men who have altered from their true nature. In fact there is no comparison between them because it is like comparing nothing to something. Similarly a person who is in his true nature is dearer to God than thousand who are not, without any comparison.
It must therefore be noted that as humans we have only one struggle which is to regain our true nature and continue to maintain after wards for once we have our true nature everything good will follow us. The first part of our struggle consists in immersing ourselves in the remembrance (dhikr) of God. This is what will help us return back to God first and back to our true self second.
The second part of this struggle is safeguarding this self-integrity lest it changes.
The third part of our struggle is offer our gratitude which eventually will earn us God's pleasure (Ridhwan).

Printed in Great Britain
by Amazon